SHUBHAM MISHRA

Cyber Security Interview Q & A

First edition
Published: 12 December, 2021
ISBN: 978-93-5526-745-0

This book is dedicated to the love of my life Shivangi

Contents

Also by Shubham Mishra

Preface

The field of cyber security is constantly evolving, and the demand for skilled cyber security professionals continues to grow. With the increasing frequency and sophistication of cyber attacks, organizations need professionals who can design, implement, and manage security strategies that protect against a wide range of threats.

This book contains a collection of cyber security interview questions and answers designed to help job seekers prepare for interviews in this field. The questions cover a range of topics, including network security, cryptography, incident response, risk management, and compliance.

The answers provided in this book are intended to provide a starting point for candidates to develop their own responses. While there are many correct ways to answer interview questions, the responses in this book provide a framework for addressing common cyber security topics and may help candidates identify areas where they need further study or practice.

Whether you are an experienced cyber security professional or a recent graduate looking for your first job, the interview process can be daunting. The goal of this book is to help candidates prepare for interviews and feel more confident in their ability to demonstrate their skills and knowledge.

As the field of cyber security continues to grow and evolve, the need for qualified professionals will only increase. We hope that this book will help job seekers in their pursuit of a fulfilling and rewarding career in cyber security.

Acknowledgement

Writing a book is a challenging endeavor, and this cyber security Q & A book would not have been possible without the contributions and support of many individuals.

Firstly, I extend my sincere gratitude to **My Parents, <u>Mr. A.K. Mishra</u> and <u>Mrs. Mamta Mishra</u>**, for believing in my abilities. Without their unwavering support and encouragement, it would not have been possible to write this book.

I am grateful to **Shivangi Dwivedi** for motivating and inspiring me to write this book.

I am pleased to **Team Pothi** (https://www.pothi.com) for their priceless support & construction advice for the primary or first publication of this book.

It is a significant challenge to produce a book of this kind, especially without the aid of divine intervention.

Finally, I would like to express my appreciation to the readers of this book, who are the ultimate beneficiaries of my collective efforts. I hope that this book will serve as a useful resource for anyone interested in learning more about cyber security and help to increase awareness of the importance of information security in today's digital age.

Shubham Mishra

About the Author

Shubham Mishra is India's youngest cybersecurity expert and a leading name in the field of ethical hacking. He is the founder and CEO of TOAE Security Solutions and has dedicated his life to the robust development of cybersecurity methods that are being used worldwide. Shubham has worked with some of the largest companies in the world for more than a decade and continues to provide updated and relevant content for the industry.

You can connect with me on:

- https://www.shubhammishra.co.in
- https://twitter.com/shubmishra07
- https://www.facebook.com/shubhammishraofficial07
- https://www.instagram.com/shub7mishra
- https://www.linkedin.com/in/shubham-mishra07

Who this book is for

This book is designed to cater to the needs of a wide range of professionals, including security experts, security architects, cyber security engineers, penetration testers, information security consultants, and incident managers. These professionals require comprehensive knowledge and understanding of the latest cyber security trends, tools, and techniques to effectively address the evolving threat landscape.

Additionally, this book aims to serve as a useful resource for novice readers and aspiring cyber security professionals who seek to learn about the latest company standards, interview questions, and procedures

I

INTRODUCTION

Cyber security refers to the practice of protecting computer systems, networks, and sensitive information from unauthorized access, theft, and damage. It includes various technologies, processes, and practices that are designed to secure the cyberspace and prevent cyber attacks.

Chapter 1

Ever since the inception of the internet, the importance of protecting your data has become more critical due to the amount of information being collected digitally. Coordinated cybercrime is quickly turning into an issue that security firms are battling to retaliate against. Many companies are recruiting experienced developers to carry out attacks against their victims. This is the place where the universe of network protection becomes an integral factor. Cyber security is a rapidly growing field that has plenty of career options, in this book we will talk about the various job interview questions asked in this field and give you an idea of what cyber security is and how it can benefit you.

Cyber security is a broad field that encompasses various techniques and procedures used to protect the integrity of multiple networks and programs. Securing the devices and networks of businesses that use them has become an essential part of their overall cybersecurity strategy. As the number of threats has increased, so has the complexity of keeping their data secure. Cybersecurity is a fast-growing industry, and it is constantly looking to keep up with the latest developments in technology. If you are good at it, you will be in a great position to stand out. Sensitive information is often the target of cyberattacks, in which criminals use this information to try and steal money from users or disrupt processes. Cyber security is used to prevent unauthorized access to sensitive information.

Types of Cyber Security Jobs

Overall, all enterprises are searching for expanded security and better assurance due to digital dangers advancing into refined and complex assaults. Also, as the business keeps on developing, more jobs are being made to fulfill the particular needs of each issue. Likewise, in any industry, there are junior and senior jobs. What's more, similarly likewise with different businesses, what you can present in experience and abilities will direct where you end up. Any place you end up, it is significant that there is incredible vocation movement in network protection, with the chance to move gradually up to better jobs.

Let's have a look at just a few of the different jobs you can find in cyber security.

1. Security software developer

2. Cryptographer

3. Ethical hacker

4. Digital forensics expert

5. Chief Information Security Officer

II

CORE INFORMATION SECURITY

Information Security is a bunch of practices expected to keep information secure from unapproved access or changes, both when it's being put away and when it's being communicated starting with one machine or actual area and then onto the next. You may now and again see it alluded to as information security. As information has become one of the 21st century's most significant resources, endeavors to keep data secure have correspondingly become progressively significant.

Chapter 2

"I think people make their own faces, as they grow."

—Enid Blyton

Q1 Can you provide a summary of information security and how it can be achieved?

Information security is the practice of protecting information and information systems from unauthorized access, use, disclosure, disruption, modification, or destruction. It can be achieved through a combination of technical, physical, and administrative controls such as access controls, firewalls, encryption, regular audits, security awareness training, and incident response planning. A strong information security program requires ongoing evaluation and adaptation to stay ahead of evolving threats.

Q2 Define the core principles of information security?

The core principles of information security are confidentiality, integrity, and availability (CIA triad). Confidentiality ensures that only authorized parties have access to sensitive information. Integrity ensures that data remains unaltered and reliable. Availability ensures that authorized users have access to information when needed. Additionally, non-repudiation is often considered a fourth principle, ensuring that actions cannot be denied by the parties involved.

Q3 What is the CIA triangle?

The CIA triangle is a widely recognized model in the field of information security that represents the three fundamental principles of information security: confidentiality, integrity, and availability.

1. Confidentiality refers to the protection of sensitive information from unauthorized access or disclosure.

2. Integrity refers to the protection of the accuracy and completeness of the information.

3. Availability refers to the assurance that information and systems are available when needed.

Q4 Define non-repudiation with reference to IT security?

1. Non-repudiation is an assurance that something is not being used or manipulated.

2. Non-repudiation is an integral part of information security. It is a legal concept that pertains to the integrity of data.

3. Every service or process that touches a piece of information should have the necessary proof of its integrity, such as a signature. This ensures that the data is secure and accurate.

Q5 Are information security and data availability relatable? If Yes explain how?

Yes, information security and data availability are related. Ensuring the security of information means protecting it from unauthorized access, modification, or destruction, which in turn ensures its availability to authorized users when needed. For example, if a system or network is hacked, it may result in the loss of data or the system being unavailable, making the data inaccessible to authorized users. Therefore, information security is crucial in maintaining the availability of data.

Q6 Can you provide an example to distinguish between logical and physical security?

1. Physical security and logical security are two key components of protecting people. Physical security measures ensure that only authorized individuals are allowed to enter a building. Logical security measures protect the data and computers of people from unauthorized access.
2. Physical security refers to the process of protecting a computer system from unauthorized access. It can be done by installing fences, alarms, and security guards. Logical security prevents unauthorized users from accessing computer software. It does so by implementing various security measures such as passwords, authentication, and encryption.
3. The contrast between logical security and physical security is logical security ensures admittance to PC frameworks and physical security protects the site and everything situated inside the site.

Q7 What are the most prevalent types of attacks that endanger enterprise data security?

- Scripting attacks (XSS, cross-site forgery)
- Injection Attacks (SQL/ javascript)
- Insider Threats
- Ransomware
- Malware that enables data exfiltration

Q8 Please provide a list of common security vulnerabilities?

- Poor Encryption/ No Encryption
- Misconfigured firewall rules
- Poor access control
- Cross-Site Scripting
- SQL Injections
- Cross-Site Forgery
- Buffer Overflows

Q9 Can you provide your opinion regarding social networking platforms such as Facebook and LinkedIn?

Facebook and LinkedIn have become an integral part of our daily lives and have revolutionized the way we communicate and connect with others. While they provide numerous benefits, such as networking opportunities and sharing information, they also come with potential risks related to privacy and security. It is crucial for individuals to take steps to protect their personal information and be mindful of the information they share online. Similarly, companies and organizations that utilize these platforms must also ensure they have proper security measures in place to protect their employees and customers sensitive data

Q10 What is the reason for internal threats being more effective than external threats?

Internal threats are often more effective than external threats because insiders generally have a greater level of access to an organization's sensitive information and systems. Insiders may have legitimate access to systems and data, such as employees or contractors, or they may be authorized individuals who misuse their access for malicious purposes.

Q11 What is the reason behind data not being completely erased when you delete it?

The reason behind data not being completely erased when you delete it is that when you delete a file, the operating system typically marks the space occupied by the file as available for reuse. However, until that space is overwritten with new data, the original file content can potentially be recovered using various file recovery tools or techniques. This is why data deletion is not considered a reliable method for permanently removing sensitive data. To ensure data is completely erased, secure data wiping techniques, such as overwriting or degaussing, should be used.

Q12 What measures would you take to ensure the permanent elimination of the risk of unauthorized access to sensitive data?

In case information is on actual media like a diskette, compact disc, or even paper, there are shredders, pulverizers, and destroyers that can transform plastic and paper into dust. For a hard drive, it's a bit tricky; The method involves taking apart the disks and wiping them clean. This method works by taking apart the platters and then degaussing them using a high-powered magnet. It prevents the data from being recovered through conventional methods.

Q13 Have you encountered any security management frameworks, such as ISO/IEC 27002, during your professional experience or training?

Yes, ISO/IEC 27002 is a security management framework that provides guidelines for organizational information security management practices. It covers a broad range of topics including risk management, access control, incident management, and more. It is widely used as a benchmark for information security management, particularly in the context of compliance and regulatory requirements.

Q14 Differentiate between a vulnerability and a threat?

A vulnerability is a weakness in a system, facility, or process that allows a threat to gain unauthorized access to it. A threat is an entity or process that uses a compromised system to perform unauthorized actions.

Q15 Explain the security policy and why it is needed?

It is a document that specifies how, when, and why people are permitted to interact with information systems. It sets acceptable expectations for users' roles and obligations, as well as provides direction for procedural tasks.

Q 16 Is there a level of risk that is deemed acceptable?

A level of risk mitigates as much risk as possible while still enabling the business to operate at optimum levels. The risk assignment should always be re-evaluated as new technologies, processes, and the threat environment changes.

Q 17 Can you briefly discuss the role of information security in each phase of the software development lifecycle?

Here's a brief overview of the role of information security in each phase of the software development lifecycle:

1. **Requirements gathering:** During this phase, security requirements are identified and documented. These requirements will be used to ensure that the system is designed and built to meet the organization's security needs.

2. **Design:** In this phase, the software architecture is designed to incorporate the security requirements identified in the previous phase. Security controls such as encryption, authentication, and access controls are incorporated into the design.

3. **Implementation:** During the implementation phase, security controls are implemented and tested to ensure that they work as intended. Secure coding practices are followed to prevent vulnerabilities such as buffer overflows and SQL injection.

4. **Testing:** Security testing is an important aspect of the software testing phase. Vulnerability scanning, penetration testing, and other security testing methods are used to identify and address any security issues.

5. **Deployment**: Before the software is deployed, it must undergo a final security review to ensure that all security requirements have been met. Once the software is deployed, ongoing monitoring and maintenance are required to ensure that it continues to meet the organization's security needs.

Overall, information security is a crucial aspect of the software development lifecycle, as it helps ensure that the software is secure and meets the organization's security requirements.

Q 18 What is the significance of security operations in the enterprise?

A security operations center (SOC) is a well-organized and well-trained group whose objective is to monitor and enhance an organization's cybersecurity posture by preventing, detecting, evaluating, and responding to cybersecurity events utilizing technology and exact processes.

Q 19 Describe incident management?

1. IT incident management is a branch of IT service management (ITSM) in which the IT team restores service as rapidly as possible after an interruption, intending to cause the least amount of disturbance to the business possible.
2. Security incident management places a strong emphasis on swiftly resolving events, so that staff and users alike don't experience too much downtime.
3. Security incident management gives a thorough and complete perspective of any security vulnerabilities inside an IT infrastructure by recognizing, managing, documenting, and evaluating security threats or incidents in real time.

Q20 DNS monitoring is important. Why?

When it comes to connecting end-users to the internet, DNS is essential. The DNS logs keep track of each client device's connection to a domain. DNS communication between client devices and your local resolver can expose information for forensic research as well as malicious activity/connections on your network, such as:

1. Malicious domains
2. Dynamic domains
3. Botnets

4. DDOS attack detection

Q21 Define security control and also list out its types?

Security control is a preventative measure used to avoid, detect, counteract, or minimize security risks. Security controls are categorized into three types

1. Logical Security Controls
2. Physical Security Controls
3. Procedural Security Controls

Q22 What do you know about Information Security Governance?

- IT security governance refers to the system that a company uses to direct and regulate IT security (adapted from ISO 38500).
- Governance defines the accountability structure and provides supervision to ensure that risks are appropriately mitigated, whereas management ensures that risk-mitigation policies are applied.

Q23 What are your professional values? Why is professional ethics crucial in the realm of information security?

When you have a huge amount of power, you also have a lot of responsibility. Security specialists are typically granted unprecedented access to company IT infrastructure and are immensely trusted. It is critical that security professionals operate ethically and honestly in order to safeguard the organization and its stakeholders.

III

PENETRATION TESTING

Penetration testing, also known as pen testing, is a simulated cyber attack on a computer system or network to identify vulnerabilities that could be exploited by attackers. The process involves testing various security measures such as firewalls, intrusion detection systems, and other security controls to identify weaknesses. Penetration testing can be done manually or using automated tools. It includes a range of activities such as reconnaissance, vulnerability identification, exploitation, and reporting. The goal of penetration testing is to identify weaknesses before malicious attackers can exploit them, and to provide recommendations for remediation. It is an essential component of an effective cybersecurity strategy.

Chapter 3

"The best teacher in life is experience."
— **LeBron James**

Q1 Define pentesting?

Penetration testing or pentesting is a security practice where a cybersecurity expert endeavors to discover and take advantage of weaknesses in a computer framework. The motivation behind this assault is to distinguish any shaky areas in a framework that attackers can exploit.

Q2 Define the primary purpose of pentesting?

A pentest is a process utilized for gaining access to an organization's electronic assets. Its goal is to find out if there are any weaknesses in the organization's infrastructure that could allow an attacker to gain unauthorized access to its systems.

Q3 What are the objectives of conducting a pentesting?

The main objectives are as follows:

1. **To identify vulnerabilities:** The main goal of pentesting is to identify vulnerabilities in an organization's systems, networks, and applications.

2. **To assess the effectiveness of security controls:** Pentesting helps to assess the effectiveness of an organization's security controls, such as firewalls, intrusion detection systems, and access controls.
3. **To measure the organization's overall security posture:** A pentesting exercise can provide a comprehensive assessment of an organization's overall security posture.

Q4 Differentiate between Vulnerability Testing and Pentesting?

In Vulnerability testing, one is just looking for any weaknesses that may exist in the infrastructure of an organization.

In pentesting, a hacker launches a full-scale digital assault or series of digital assaults is dispatched with express consent from the client to explicitly discover any sorts of holes that have not yet been found by the IT security team.

Q5 Describe in detail three types of pentesting methodologies?

The three types are as follows:

- Black-Box Testing
- White-Box Testing
- Gray-Box Testing

1. Black-Box Testing

In black-box testing, the hacker might have very little or no knowledge about their target. So with an end goal to attempt to get through the lines of protection, the hacker will use Brute Force Attack. This kind of testing is also known as a trial-and-error approach. Black-box testing is usually performed by automated tools as it requires a huge amount of time.

2. White-Box Testing

In white-box testing, the attacker has an advanced knowledge of the Web application they are about to attack. It is also known as clear-box testing. This attack is less time-consuming compared to black-box testing.

3. Gray-Box Testing

Gray-box testing is an advanced form of testing that consists of both black-box and white-box tests. It gives the testers the most advanced knowledge on the various targets they plan to attack. This sort of testing requires both automated and manual tools. It can also be very useful for security researchers since it can detect weaknesses and security holes that are usually missed by the other two testings.

Q6 Explain the teams that carry out penetration testing?

The teams are as follows:

- The Red Team
- The Blue Team
- The Purple Team

1. The Red Team

A red team is a group of skilled professionals who simulate an attack on an organization's systems and applications. They use a range of techniques and tools to identify vulnerabilities and weaknesses that could be exploited by attackers.

2. The Blue Team

A blue team is a group of defenders who are responsible for detecting and responding to attacks. They use a range of tools and techniques to monitor the organization's systems and applications and identify any unusual activity.

3. The Purple Team

The purple team is a blend of the red and blue teams. They work together to simulate attacks and test the organization's defenses. The purple team approach emphasizes collaboration and knowledge sharing between the red and blue teams.

Q7 Which certifications are most in demand for penetration testing?

To be recognized as a top pentester in the cybersecurity field, there are certain certifications that are considered essential

1. **Certified Ethical Hacker (CEH):** Offered by EC-Council, the CEH certification validates an individual's knowledge of ethical hacking methodologies and tools.
2. **Offensive Security Certified Professional (OSCP):** Offered by Offensive Security, the OSCP certification is widely recognized as one of the most rigorous and challenging certifications in the field of penetration testing. It demonstrates an individual's ability to identify vulnerabilities and successfully exploit them.
3. **GIAC Penetration Tester (GPEN):** Offered by GIAC, the GPEN certification validates an individual's ability to conduct a thorough and effective penetration test.

Q8 When presenting the results of a pentesting, it is important to communicate the findings not only to the IT staff but also to the C-level executives, who may have limited technical knowledge. How would you effectively explain the results to them?

When communicating the results of a pentesting to C-level executives, it is important to strike a balance between technical accuracy and clear communication. By presenting the findings in a way that is easy to understand and highlighting the most critical vulnerabilities, you can help the executives make informed decisions about how to improve the organization's security posture. The pentesting reports should include a risk analysis that demonstrates the financial impact of any vulnerabilities that are discovered and not addressed. The report should also include financial calculations that demonstrate the potential costs of a security breach.

Q9 Explain cross-site scripting?

Cross-site scripting (XSS) is a type of security vulnerability that allows an attacker to inject malicious scripts into a web page viewed by other users, which can be used to steal sensitive information or control the user's session.

Q10 Can you explain what data packet sniffing is and provide examples of some commonly used tools for this purpose?

Data packet sniffing is the practice of intercepting and analyzing data packets that flow across a network. It is often used by security professionals to detect security vulnerabilities or troubleshoot network issues.

Some widely used tools for packet sniffing include Wireshark, tcpdump, and Microsoft Network Monitor. These tools capture and analyze network traffic, allowing security professionals to identify patterns or anomalies in the data, which can help them to identify security threats or network issues.

Q11 Please provide the full expansions of the following abbreviations that are commonly used in pentesting: 2FA, 2S2D, 2VPCP, 3DES, 3DESE, 3DESEP?

The acronyms stand for the following:

- 2FA means "Two-Factor Authentication"
- 2SD2D means "Double-Sided, Double Density"
- 2VPCP means "Two-Version Priority Ceiling Protocol"
- 3DES means "Triple Data Encryption Standard"
- 3DESE means "Triple Data Encryption Standard Encryption"
- 3DESEP means "Triple Data Encryption Standard Encryption Protocol"

Q12 What are the typical network security weaknesses that a pentester encounters?

Some of the most common network security vulnerabilities that a pentester may come across include weak passwords, unpatched software, and operating systems, misconfigured firewalls, lack of encryption, vulnerable applications, and social engineering attacks. Other vulnerabilities may include open ports, outdated protocols, and unauthorized access to sensitive information.

Q13 What are the various techniques used in pentesting?

Pentesting techniques fall into the following categories:

- Web Application Testing
- Wireless Network/Wireless Device Testing
- Network Infrastructure Services
- Social Engineering Testing
- Client-Side Application Testing

Q14 Which network ports are frequently analyzed during a pentesting, and what is the tool used for this purpose?

During a pentesting exercise, commonly examined network ports include HTTP (port 80), HTTPS (port 443), SSH (port 22), Telnet (port 23), FTP (port 21), and DNS (port 53). Port scanning tools, such as Nmap, can be used to identify open ports on a target network or system.

Q15 Can you provide a detailed explanation of what SQL injection is?

SQL injection is a type of cyber attack in which an attacker injects malicious SQL statements into a vulnerable website or application, allowing them to bypass security measures and gain unauthorized access to sensitive data or manipulate the database.

Q16 Can you explain the main distinction between asymmetric and symmetric cryptography and provide an example of the former?

The main distinction between asymmetric and symmetric cryptography is that symmetric cryptography uses the same key for both encryption and decryption, while asymmetric cryptography uses a different key for each process.

An example of asymmetric cryptography is the RSA algorithm, which uses a public key to encrypt data and a private key to decrypt it. The public key is widely distributed and can be used by anyone to encrypt data that can only be decrypted by the owner of the private key. This allows secure communication without the need for both parties to share a secret key.

Q17 How many permutations are required for a robust SSL connection to be established?

The following characteristics are required:

- The session identifier
- A peer certificate
- An established compression method
- Any associated cipher specs

Q18 What are SSL and TSL?

SSL (Secure Sockets Layer) and TLS (Transport Layer Security) are cryptographic protocols that are used to provide secure communication over a computer network. They provide encryption, data integrity, and authentication services to protect the confidentiality and integrity of data transmitted between devices. SSL was the predecessor of TLS and both are commonly used for secure communication over the internet, such as secure web browsing (HTTPS).

IV

NETWORKING

Networking refers to the practice of connecting devices, systems, and other components to enable communication and data exchange. It involves the use of hardware and software components, including network protocols, routers, switches, firewalls, and other network devices, to establish, maintain, and manage a network. Networking is essential for businesses, organizations, and individuals to access resources, share information, and collaborate efficiently. It also enables remote access to systems and data, which has become increasingly important in the era of cloud computing and remote work. Effective networking requires knowledge of network architecture, security protocols, network troubleshooting, and other related concepts.

Chapter 4

"If you spend more on coffee than on IT security, you will be hacked."

—Richard Clarke

Q1 Define firewall?

A firewall is a security device that decides which traffic can be allowed or blocked on the network. It enforces rules based on the security policies of the network.

Q2 In addition to firewalls, what other network security devices are used to establish network boundaries?

Beyond perimeter security devices, other devices such as network access points and load balancers can also improve network performance.

Q3 What is the function of network boundaries in ensuring information security?

Network boundaries are a crucial aspect of information security as they help in defining the limits of a network and control the flow of information in and out of it. A network boundary can be a physical or virtual separation between different networks or parts of a network that are secured to varying degrees. By enforcing security measures such as firewalls and access controls at the network boundary, an organization can protect its systems and data from unauthorized access and other cyber threats that may originate from outside the network.

Q4 Explain intrusion detection (IDS) systems?

Intrusion Detection Systems (IDS) are security technologies that monitor network or system activities to detect and prevent unauthorized access, policy violations, and malicious activities. IDS alerts security teams when suspicious or unauthorized activities are detected, enabling them to take appropriate action to protect critical information assets.

Q5 Explain honeypot? What type of attack does it defend against?

A honeypot is a decoy system or network designed to attract and distract attackers, allowing security teams to monitor their behavior and learn from their tactics. Honeypots can be configured to simulate vulnerable systems or applications to attract attackers looking for potential targets to exploit. By luring attackers away from real systems and applications, honeypots can provide early warning of attacks and enable security teams to proactively defend against them. Honeypots can defend against various types of attacks, such as malware, ransomware, and phishing, by providing a controlled environment to study the attacker's tactics and gather threat intelligence.

Q6 Explain the working of packet filtering?

Packet filtering is a network security technique that selectively blocks or allows network traffic based on predefined rules. When a packet is received, the packet filtering firewall compares it to a set of rules to determine if it should be allowed through or blocked. The rules can be based on various parameters such as the source and destination IP addresses, port numbers, and protocols. If the packet meets the criteria specified in the rules, it is allowed to pass through; otherwise, it is dropped or rejected.

Q7 Can you provide a brief overview of IP multicast?

IP multicast is a networking technology that allows one-to-many or many-to-many communication over an IP network. It enables efficient transmission of data to multiple recipients simultaneously, reducing network traffic and improving bandwidth utilization. IP multicast is widely used in multimedia streaming, video conferencing, and content delivery networks.

Q8 Differentiate between a packet filtering firewall and an application layer firewall?

Packet filtering firewalls and application layer firewalls are two types of network security technologies, and the main difference between them is their level of protection and functionality.

Packet filtering firewalls operate at the network layer of the OSI model, which means they examine packets at the IP and transport layer to determine whether to allow or block traffic based on predefined rules. They are generally fast and efficient, but they lack the ability to inspect the content of packets or data payloads.

On the other hand, application layer firewalls operate at the application layer of the OSI model, which means they can analyze the content of packets to identify specific applications or protocols and their associated risks. They can also perform deep packet inspection to detect and block application-level attacks such as SQL injection and cross-site scripting (XSS).

Application layer firewalls are more sophisticated than packet filtering firewalls and provide a higher level of protection, but they are also slower and more resource-intensive.

Q9 What are the layers of the OSI model?

The 7 Layers of the OSI

- Layer 7 - Application.
- Layer 6 - Presentation.
- Layer 5 - Session.
- Layer 4 - Transport.
- Layer 3 - Network.
- Layer 2 - Data Link.
- Layer 1 - Physical.

Q10 If there is a breakdown in communication, how would you detect it using traceroute?

Traceroute is a network diagnostic tool that can help detect breakdowns in communication by tracing the path of packets from the source to the destination. If there is a breakdown in communication, traceroute may show a packet loss or a significant increase in latency or response time at a particular hop along the path, indicating a potential issue or bottleneck in the network. Additionally, if the traceroute is unable to reach the destination, it may suggest a complete failure in communication.

Q11 What are the benefits of using a firewall?

Firewalls provide many benefits to organizations and individual users, including:

1. **Network security:** Firewalls protect against unauthorized access to networks and systems by filtering incoming and outgoing traffic based on predefined rules.
2. **Threat detection:** Firewalls can detect and block known and unknown threats, such as malware, viruses, and other types of malicious traffic.
3. **Access control:** Firewalls can enforce access control policies to restrict access to sensitive resources and applications based on user identity, role, or other criteria.
4. **Improved network performance:** Firewalls can improve network performance by optimizing traffic flow, reducing network congestion, and blocking unwanted traffic.
5. **Compliance:** Firewalls can help organizations comply with regulatory requirements by enforcing security policies, protecting sensitive data, and providing audit trails.
6. **Peace of mind:** Firewalls provide peace of mind by protecting against cyber threats and ensuring the confidentiality, integrity, and availability of critical information assets.

Q12 Explain Proxy firewall?

A proxy firewall is a type of firewall that operates at the application layer of the OSI model and acts as an intermediary between the user and the internet. It intercepts all requests from the user and forwards them on behalf of the user to the internet, allowing the user to remain anonymous and providing an additional layer of security by blocking or filtering traffic based on predefined rules.

Q13 Active FTP does not work with network firewalls. Why?

Active FTP uses two separate channels for data transfer: one for control information and another for data transmission. The control channel uses TCP port 21, while the data channel uses a dynamically assigned port above 1023. When a client initiates an Active FTP transfer, the FTP server sends a connection request back to the client on the dynamically assigned port, which is typically blocked by network firewalls for security reasons.

As a result, Active FTP may not work with network firewalls that block incoming connections from unknown ports. This issue can be addressed by configuring the firewall to allow incoming connections on the dynamically assigned port or by using a passive FTP mode, which uses a single port for both control and data transfer and is better suited for use with firewalls.

Q14 Explain Administrator Privileges?

Administrator privileges refer to the level of access granted to a user account in a computer system or network, allowing the user to perform tasks that are typically restricted to other users, such as installing software, modifying system files, and managing user accounts. However, these privileges also pose security risks if granted to unauthorized users.

Q15 Describe intranet?

An intranet is a private network within an organization that uses Internet protocols and technologies to share information, collaboration tools, and computing resources among its members. Unlike the public Internet, access to an intranet is typically restricted to authorized users within the organization and can include features such as email, file sharing, document management, and internal websites.

Q16 How would you create a checksum?

The following steps are involved in creating the checksum:

- Divide the data into sections
- Add the sections together using 1's complement arithmetic
- Take the complement of the final sum

Q17 What is simplex? Can you provide one example of it?

Simplex is a method of data transmission in which the communication occurs in one direction only, from the sender to the receiver. It is a one-way communication mode that does not allow for feedback or response from the receiver.

One example of simplex communication is a television broadcast, where the signal is transmitted from the broadcast station to the viewers. The viewers can receive the signal but cannot send any feedback or response to the station.

Q18 Define RIP?

Routing Information Protocol (RIP) is a distance-vector routing protocol used in IP networks to automatically exchange routing information among routers. RIP uses hop count as a metric to determine the best path to a destination network and has a limit of 15 hops.

Q19 What are the factors affecting network performance?

The factors that affect the performance of the network are:

- Type of transmission media
- Software
- Number of users
- Hardware

Q20 Why TCP is used in the IP packets?

TCP (Transmission Control Protocol) is used in IP packets to provide reliable, ordered, and error-checked delivery of data between applications running on different hosts over a network. TCP ensures that data packets are transmitted and received correctly, and in the correct sequence.

Q21 Explain the errors in data communication over a network

There are two types of errors:

1. **Single-bit Error:** A single-bit error is a type of data transmission error where only one bit in a block of data is changed during transmission, resulting in the corruption of that bit's value
2. **Burst Error:** A burst error is a type of error that occurs when two or more bits in a data transmission are changed due to a single error in the transmission medium, such as electromagnetic interference or noise.

Q22 Explain ALOHA?

ALOHA is a system for coordinating and arbitrating access to a shared communication network channel. It is often used to solve the channel allocation issue. Two types of ALOHA are:

1. **Pure Aloha** protocol is a random access protocol for media access control in a network. In Pure Aloha, a device transmits data whenever it has data to send, without checking for other transmissions on the network. If two devices transmit at the same time, a collision occurs and both devices must retransmit later. Pure Aloha is simple to implement, but it suffers from high collision rates and low network efficiency.

2. **Slotted Aloha** is an improved version of Pure Aloha. It divides time into slots and devices are only allowed to transmit at the beginning of each slot. This reduces the probability of collision and increases network efficiency. However, Slotted Aloha requires more synchronization between devices and can lead to wasted slots if a device has no data to transmit.

Q23 How many bits are required to represent a subnet size?

The number of bits required for a subnet size depends on the number of hosts that need to be accommodated in the subnet. Each additional bit in the subnet mask doubles the number of possible subnets while halving the number of possible hosts in each subnet. For example, a subnet with 256 hosts requires 8 bits ($2^8=256$), while a subnet with 64 hosts requires 6 bits ($2^6=64$). Generally, it is recommended to use the minimum number of bits required to accommodate the number of hosts needed in the subnet, in order to conserve IP address space.

V

NETWORK SECURITY

Network security refers to the measures and technologies that are implemented to protect computer networks and data from unauthorized access, attacks, and data breaches. It encompasses the policies, procedures, and tools designed to ensure the confidentiality, integrity, and availability of network data and resources. Network security strategies may include firewalls, intrusion detection and prevention systems, virtual private networks (VPNs), secure sockets layer (SSL) and transport layer security (TLS) encryption, and access control systems. The goal of network security is to provide a secure computing environment that enables authorized users to access network resources while preventing unauthorized users from accessing sensitive data or causing network disruptions.

Chapter 5

"I get hired to hack into computers now and sometimes it's actually easier than it was years ago."

— Kevin Mitnick

Q1 Over which port does the ping command work?

Ping doesn't work over a specific port number, as it's a network utility that uses the Internet Control Message Protocol (ICMP) to test the reachability of a network host and to measure the round-trip time for packets sent from the source host to the destination host. ICMP is a protocol that operates at the network layer of the OSI model, and it's not associated with any particular port.

Q2 Would you rather have ports on your firewall filtered or closed?

The choice between the two depends on the specific security needs of the network and the organization. Filtered ports allow certain types of traffic to pass through while blocking others, while closed ports completely block all traffic. Both have their advantages and disadvantages, and the decision depends on the specific network configuration and security requirements.

Q3 Can you explain the underlying protocol mechanism of traceroute/tracert?

TTraceroute/tracert works by sending packets with gradually increasing Time To Live (TTL) values to the target host. Each router along the path decrements the TTL value by 1 and discards the packet when the TTL reaches 0, sending an ICMP error message back to the source host. By analyzing the sequence of ICMP error messages received, traceroute/tracert can identify the routers along the path and measure the time taken for each packet to travel between the source and destination hosts.

Q4 In what ways does Linux excel and fall short in comparison to Windows?

Advantages:

- Mostly Free
- Mostly Open Source
- Very Stable
- Extensive Configuration Possibilities

Disadvantages:

- Limited Range of Software
- Significant barriers to entry for those with little IT knowledge

Q5 What methods and technologies are utilized to ensure the security of information and services that are deployed on cloud computing infrastructure?

Securing information and services on cloud computing infrastructure involves a range of technologies and approaches, including access controls, encryption, firewalls, intrusion detection and prevention, network segmentation, and regular vulnerability scanning and patching. It also involves establishing clear security policies and procedures and training users on best practices for securing their data and systems.

Q6 What are the information security challenges that one can encounter in a cloud computing environment?

Cloud computing offers numerous benefits, such as scalability, flexibility, and cost savings, but it also presents several information security challenges that organizations must address. Here are some of the key challenges:

1. **Data security:** Cloud computing involves storing and processing data on shared infrastructure, which can increase the risk of data breaches and unauthorized access. Organizations must implement strong access controls, encryption, and monitoring to protect sensitive data.
2. **Compliance and regulatory issues:** Cloud computing poses challenges to compliance with regulations such as HIPAA, GDPR, and PCI DSS. Organizations must ensure that their cloud infrastructure and services meet the requirements of these regulations and that they have adequate controls in place to protect sensitive data.
3. **Lack of visibility and control:** Cloud infrastructure is often complex and dynamic, making it difficult for organizations to monitor and control their cloud environment. This can lead to security blind spots and vulnerabilities that are difficult to detect and mitigate.
4. **Insider threats:** Cloud computing introduces new risks related to insider

threats, such as unauthorized access and data exfiltration. Organizations must implement strong access controls, monitoring, and employee training to mitigate these risks.

5. **Third-party risks:** Cloud computing involves working with third-party providers, which introduces new risks related to supply chain security, vendor management, and data ownership. Organizations must carefully evaluate and manage their relationships with cloud providers to mitigate these risks.

Q7 What are the steps to log in to Active Directory from a Linux or Mac computer?

To log in to Active Directory from a Linux or Mac box, you would need to use a tool such as Samba, which provides an implementation of the Server Message Block (SMB) protocol used by Windows and Active Directory. You would need to configure Samba with the appropriate settings for your Active Directory domain, including the domain name, user credentials, and LDAP server settings. Once configured, you can use the "smbclient" command to connect to and authenticate with the Active Directory domain.

Q8 How can you configure a network to restrict login access to only a single computer on a specific jack?

One easy way to configure a network to allow only a single computer to log in on a particular jack is to use port security. Port security is a feature found on many network switches that allows administrators to restrict access to a particular network port based on the MAC address of the connected device.

To configure port security, you would first need to determine the MAC address of the authorized device. You can then log in to the switch and configure the port security settings for the relevant network port, specifying the MAC address of the authorized device as the only allowed address.

Once port security is enabled, any attempt to connect another device to the port will result in the port being automatically disabled or placed in a "shutdown" state, preventing unauthorized access to the network. If the authorized device is disconnected or replaced, the port will need to be reconfigured with the new MAC address to allow access.

Q9 Can you list the three methods of authenticating a person?

There are generally three ways to authenticate a person:

1. **Something you know:** This is a knowledge-based authentication method, such as a password, PIN, or security question. The user must provide the correct answer to gain access to a system or resource.
2. **Something you have:** This is a possession-based authentication method, such as a smart card, token, or mobile device. The user must have the physical device in their possession to gain access.
3. **Something you are:** This is a biometric authentication method, such as a fingerprint, facial recognition, or iris scan. The user must provide a biometric sample that matches the stored biometric data to gain access.

Each of these authentication methods has its own strengths and weaknesses, and organizations often use a combination of methods to provide multiple layers of security. For example, a system may require a password (something you know) and a fingerprint scan (something you are) to authenticate a user.

Q10 In terms of firewall detection, which is more serious - a false negative or a false positive, and what is the reason for this?

In firewall detection, a false negative is generally worse than a false positive. A false negative occurs when an attack or unauthorized access is not detected by the firewall and is allowed to pass through, potentially causing damage or compromise of the system or network. In contrast, a false positive occurs when legitimate traffic or activity is incorrectly flagged as malicious or unauthorized, causing inconvenience but not necessarily resulting in a security breach.

Q11 Can you explain how to determine whether a remote server is running IIS or Apache?

There are several ways to determine if a remote server is running IIS or Apache:

1. **Use a web browser:** Visiting the remote server's IP address or domain name in a web browser may reveal information about the web server software being used.
2. **Use a tool such as "curl" or "wget":** These tools can be used to make HTTP requests to the remote server and may reveal information about the web server software being used.
3. **Use a network scanner:** Tools such as "nmap" can be used to scan the remote server and identify open ports and services, including the web server software being used.
4. **Inspect HTTP response headers:** Tools such as "telnet" or "netcat" can be used to connect to the remote server and issue HTTP requests, allowing inspection of the response headers, which may include information about the web server software being used.

Q12 Differentiate between a HIDS and a NIDS?

A HIDS (Host-based Intrusion Detection System) is a security system that is installed on a single host or server, and it monitors activity on that system to detect suspicious or malicious activity. HIDS typically use system logs and file integrity checking to identify potential intrusions.

A NIDS (Network-based Intrusion Detection System) is a security system that is deployed on a network to monitor and analyze network traffic for potential security breaches. NIDS typically uses network packets to detect and respond to security threats, such as network scans, denial-of-service attacks, and unauthorized access attempts.

The main difference between the two is that HIDS focuses on monitoring the activity of a single host, while NIDS focuses on monitoring the traffic flowing through a network.

Q13 Differentiate between closed-source and open-source? Which is better?

Closed-source software is proprietary software that is developed by a company or individual and distributed under a license that restricts access to the source code. Only the compiled executable is made available to users.

Open-source software is software that is developed collaboratively by a community of developers, and the source code is freely available for anyone to use, modify, and distribute under the terms of the applicable open-source license.

It's difficult to say which is better, as both have their advantages and disadvantages. Closed-source software tends to be more polished and well-documented, with dedicated support from the developers. However, it can be more expensive and may not be customizable to the same degree as open-source software. Open-source software is typically more customizable, and since the source code is available, it can be audited for security vulnerabilities by anyone. However, it may be less user-friendly and may not have the same level of support as commercial software.

Ultimately, the choice between closed-source and open-source software will depend on the specific needs and preferences of the user or organization.

Q14 What steps would you take to secure a mobile device?

Here are some steps to lock down a mobile device:

1. Set a strong passcode or password.
2. Enable biometric authentication, if available.
3. Disable unnecessary app permissions and location tracking.
4. Enable automatic OS updates.
5. Install and regularly update antivirus software.
6. Use a virtual private network (VPN) to encrypt network traffic.
7. Only install apps from trusted sources.
8. Regularly backup the device data.
9. Use remote wipe capabilities in case the device is lost or stolen.

Q15 Explain exfiltration?

Exfiltration is the unauthorized transfer of data from an organization's internal network or computer system to an external system or location. It is a type of data breach where sensitive or confidential information is extracted from the organization's network by an attacker or insider.

Exfiltrated data can include financial records, personally identifiable information, trade secrets, or other sensitive information. Attackers often use various techniques such as malware, phishing, social engineering, or exploiting vulnerabilities to gain access to the organization's network and exfiltrate data. Exfiltration is a serious security threat and can result in reputational damage, financial losses, and regulatory fines.

Q16 What are the benefits of using SSH on a Windows computer?

There are several reasons why you might want to use SSH from a Windows PC:

1. **Secure Remote Access:** SSH provides a secure method of remotely accessing servers and other devices over the internet. With SSH, you can securely manage remote servers, routers, switches, and other network devices.

2. **Encrypted File Transfers:** SSH also allows for secure file transfers between computers. You can use SSH's SFTP (Secure File Transfer Protocol) or SCP (Secure Copy Protocol) to securely transfer files over the internet.

3. **Command-Line Access:** SSH provides a command-line interface that allows you to run remote commands on another computer. This can be useful for managing servers and other devices that are not physically located near you.

4. **Tunneling:** SSH can also be used to create secure tunnels between computers, allowing you to securely access services on a remote network that are not normally accessible over the internet.

Overall, SSH is a powerful tool that can help you securely manage and access remote computers and networks from a Windows PC.

Q17 What is the method to determine the meaning of a POST code?

POST (Power-On Self Test) codes are diagnostic codes that a computer's BIOS (Basic Input/Output System) generates during the boot process. To find out what a POST code means, you can consult the documentation for the computer's BIOS. The BIOS manual should have a list of POST codes and their meanings. Alternatively, you can search for the POST code online or on the manufacturer's website to find information about what it means and how to troubleshoot the issue.

Q18 What is your source of security-related information?

Here are some common sources of security news:

1. **Tech Websites:** Many tech websites, such as TechCrunch, ZDNet, and Wired, have dedicated sections for cybersecurity news.
2. **Security Blogs:** Several security experts and companies maintain blogs where they discuss the latest security news and trends.
3. **Social Media:** Twitter, LinkedIn, and other social media platforms are also good sources of security news, where users can follow security researchers, experts, and companies.
4. **Newsletters:** Several security newsletters, such as SANS NewsBites and KrebsOnSecurity, provide regular updates on security news and trends.

Q19 Differentiate between symmetric and public-key cryptography?

Symmetric cryptography uses the same secret key for both the encryption and decryption of data. Public-key cryptography, on the other hand, uses two separate keys: a public key for encryption and a private key for decryption. This makes public-key cryptography more secure than symmetric cryptography because the private key is kept secret and not shared with anyone.

Q20 Could you describe the initial three actions you take when securing a Linux server?

Here are three common steps to secure a Linux server:

1. **Update Software:** The first step in securing a Linux server is to make sure that all software is up to date. This includes the operating system, applications, and any third-party software.
2. **Harden System:** After updating the software, the next step is to harden the system. This involves disabling unnecessary services, limiting user permissions, and implementing strong passwords.
3. **Install Firewall:** The third step is to install a firewall to control incoming and outgoing network traffic. The firewall can be configured to block unauthorized access to the server and only allow necessary services to communicate with the outside world. Additionally, it's important to regularly monitor the server's logs and update security settings as necessary.

Q21 How would you gain unauthorized access to an "office workstation" at a hotel?

Considering how infected these typically are, I wouldn't touch one with a 10ft pole. That being said, a USB keylogger is easy to fit into the back of these systems without much notice while an autorun program would be able to run quickly and quietly leaving behind software to do the dirty work. In essence, it's open season on exploits in this type of environment.

Q22 How would you ensure permanent protection of data from falling into the wrong hands?

There is only one way to 100% ensure this, destroy any and all devices the data is stored on. There are industrial shredders designed for turning hard drives into confetti.

Q23 If you come across an active problem on your network that you can fix but is outside of your jurisdiction, what actions would you take?

If there is an active problem on the network that I am not authorized to fix, I would report the issue to the appropriate person or team responsible for the network. This could include the IT department or a security team. I would provide as much detail as possible about the issue, such as the type of problem, its severity, and any potential impact on the network or users. It is important to follow established policies and procedures for reporting security incidents and to avoid attempting to fix the issue on my own without proper authorization.

Q24 What do you think of social networking sites such as Facebook and LinkedIn from a security point of view?

Social networking sites such as Facebook and LinkedIn pose some security risks that companies need to consider when using them. These sites can provide an avenue for attackers to gain access to sensitive information, such as login credentials or personal data. Additionally, employees who use these sites at work may unwittingly download malware or fall for phishing scams, which can compromise the security of the entire network.

Q25 What does an intrusion detection system do? How does it do it?

An intrusion detection system (IDS) is a security technology designed to detect and prevent unauthorized access to computer systems or networks. It does this by monitoring network traffic and system activity for suspicious behavior and events that indicate a potential security breach.

There are two types of IDS: network-based and host-based. Network-based IDS monitors network traffic and analyzes packets to identify potential security threats, while host-based IDS monitors system logs and activity on individual hosts to detect unauthorized access.

IDS uses a variety of techniques, such as signature-based detection, anomaly detection, and behavior analysis, to identify potential security threats. Once a threat is detected, IDS can trigger alerts, log events, or even take automatic actions to block or isolate the threat.

Overall, IDS is an important component of a comprehensive security strategy, helping organizations to identify and respond to potential security breaches before they can cause damage or disrupt operations.

VI

APPLICATION SECURITY

Application security refers to the measures taken to secure software applications from external threats and to prevent the exploitation of vulnerabilities in the application. The goal of application security is to ensure that applications are free from security flaws that could be exploited by attackers to gain unauthorized access to sensitive information or systems. This can include both preventing attacks from the outside, such as through firewalls and intrusion detection systems, as well as ensuring that applications are secure from the inside, through secure coding practices, input validation, and other security measures. Application security is essential for protecting both users and organizations from potential harm and financial loss.

Chapter 6

"Time is what determines security. With enough time nothing is unhackable."

—Aniekee Ezekiel

Q1 What are some ways to implement a secure login field on a high-traffic website while considering performance?

To implement a secure login field on a high-traffic website while maintaining performance, I would consider the following steps:

1. Use SSL/TLS encryption to secure communication between the user's browser and the webserver to prevent eavesdropping and man-in-the-middle attacks.
2. Implement a strong password policy with minimum length, complexity, and expiration rules to prevent brute force attacks and credential stuffing.
3. Use multi-factor authentication (MFA) to add an extra layer of security. For example, sending an SMS or push notification to the user's mobile device as a second authentication factor.
4. Implement rate limiting and IP blocking to prevent automated attacks and brute-force attempts.
5. Use caching mechanisms such as Redis or Memcached to store user sessions and reduce the load on the server.
6. Use a load balancer or content delivery network (CDN) to distribute traffic

across multiple servers and prevent overloading a single server.

7. Continuously monitor and analyze the website's traffic, logs, and security events to detect and respond to potential security incidents in real time.

By following these steps, a secure login field can be implemented on a high-traffic website while minimizing performance issues.

Q2. Can you explain the different approaches to mitigate the risk of account brute-force attacks?

There are several ways to handle account brute-forcing attacks:

1. **Implement account lockout policy:** After a certain number of failed login attempts, lock the user account for a specified period of time. This can prevent brute-force attacks and protect user accounts.
2. **Use CAPTCHA:** Implement a CAPTCHA system that requires users to prove they are human by solving a puzzle or entering a code. This can prevent automated bots from performing brute-force attacks.
3. **Implement Two-Factor Authentication:** Implement two-factor authentication, such as sending a one-time password (OTP) to the user's registered mobile device or email address as a second authentication factor, to prevent unauthorized access even if the password is compromised.
4. **Use strong passwords:** Enforce a strong password policy with minimum length, complexity, and expiration rules to prevent easy password guessing.
5. **Implement rate limiting:** Limit the number of login attempts from a specific IP address within a certain period of time to prevent brute-forcing.
6. **Use Intrusion Detection and Prevention Systems:** Deploy intrusion detection and prevention systems to detect and block brute-force attacks in real time.

By implementing these techniques, account brute-forcing attacks can be mitigated, and user accounts can be protected.

Q3 Can you provide an explanation of cross-site request forgery (CSRF) and some effective strategies to prevent it?

Cross-Site Request Forgery (CSRF) is a type of attack in which a malicious website or application tricks a user into performing an action on a different website or application that they are authenticated to, without their knowledge or consent.

The attacker can exploit the user's existing session on the targeted website, and perform actions on behalf of the user, such as making a financial transaction, changing their password, or posting content.

To defend against CSRF attacks, you can implement the following measures:

1. **Use CSRF Tokens:** Add a unique and unpredictable CSRF token to each request that can only be generated by the server. The token is verified by the server to ensure that the request was generated by a legitimate user and not an attacker.
2. **Implement SameSite Cookies:** Use the SameSite attribute in cookies to restrict the cookie from being sent in a cross-origin request.
3. **Use Anti-CSRF Libraries:** Implement anti-CSRF libraries, such as OWASP CSRFGuard, to automatically add CSRF tokens and other security measures to your web application.
4. **Enforce Strict Access Control:** Ensure that user sessions are only valid for the intended purpose and only the necessary actions can be performed, such as by implementing proper access control mechanisms.

By implementing these measures, you can defend against CSRF attacks and protect your web application and users' sensitive data.

Q4 Suppose you are a site administrator glancing for incoming CSRF attacks, what would you look for?

As a site administrator looking for incoming CSRF attacks, I would monitor the site's logs for suspicious activity, such as an unusual number of requests or attempts to access restricted resources. I would also check the referer header to see if requests are coming from unexpected sources. Additionally, I would implement CSRF protection measures such as adding a CSRF token to forms and validating that token on form submission.

Q5 Differentiate between HTTP and HTML?

HTTP (Hypertext Transfer Protocol) is a protocol used to transfer data over the web. It defines the way data is transferred between a web server and a client, such as a web browser. HTTP specifies how requests and responses should be formatted and how they should be transmitted.

HTML (Hypertext Markup Language) is a markup language used to create web pages. HTML is the language that describes the structure and content of web pages. It is used to format text, add images, and create links between web pages. HTML files are transferred over HTTP from web servers to web clients (browsers) for rendering.

Q6 How does HTTP handle state?

HTTP is stateless, which means that it does not maintain any information about the previous requests made by a client. However, HTTP cookies can be used to create stateful sessions between the client and the server. Cookies allow the server to store and retrieve information about the client, allowing the server to maintain state between requests.

Q7 How would you briefly explain to a non-IT person about cross-site scripting?

Cross-site scripting (XSS) is when an attacker injects malicious code into a website to steal user data.

Q8 Differentiate between Stored and Reflected XSS?

Stored Cross-Site Scripting (XSS) is an attack in which the malicious code is stored on the target server, and when a user visits the infected page, the script is executed.

Reflected Cross-Site Scripting (XSS), on the other hand, is an attack in which the malicious code is injected into a web page's response to the user's request, and the code is executed when the user clicks on a specially crafted link.

Q9 What are the common defenses against XSS?

The common defenses against Cross-Site Scripting (XSS) attacks include input validation and output encoding to ensure that user input is valid and safe. Properly sanitizing user input and filtering out potentially malicious code can also prevent XSS attacks. Web Application Firewalls (WAFs) can also detect and prevent attacks by filtering out malicious traffic, and Content Security Policy (CSP) headers can be used to specify which content is allowed to be loaded on a website, preventing unauthorized scripts.

Q10 Suppose you are remoted into a headless system in a distant region. You have no access to hardware and you want to install an operating system. What will be your plan of action?

In a situation where remote access is the only available option and there is no physical access to the hardware, you can perform the OS installation using a remote console or remote desktop solution. If the headless system has a remote management interface, such as IPMI or iDRAC, you can use that to remotely mount an OS image and boot the system from it.

Q11 Why is it easier to break into a local account than an AD account in a Windows network?

Breaking into a local account on a Windows network is easier than breaking into an Active Directory (AD) account because local accounts are managed and authenticated on individual computers, whereas AD accounts are managed centrally and authenticated across the entire domain. Local accounts often have weaker password policies and are not subject to the same security controls as AD accounts.

Additionally, local accounts are usually used by a single user, making them more susceptible to phishing attacks and other social engineering tactics compared to AD accounts, which can have multiple layers of authentication and authorization.

Q12 You see a user logging in as root to perform basic functions. Is this a problem?

Yes, it is generally not recommended to perform basic functions as the root user because it can potentially compromise the security of the system. The root user has unrestricted access to all system resources, so any mistakes made while using root privileges could have serious consequences. It is better to create a separate user with limited privileges and only use root when necessary for administrative tasks. This minimizes the risk of accidental or intentional damage to the system.

Q13 What is data protection in transit vs data protection at rest?

Data protection in transit refers to the security measures taken to protect data while it is being transmitted over a network or between systems. This includes using encryption protocols such as SSL/TLS to secure the data during transmission and ensuring that proper authentication and access control measures are in place to prevent unauthorized access.

Data protection at rest refers to the security measures taken to protect data while it is stored on a device or system, such as a hard drive, database, or cloud storage service. This includes using encryption to protect the data from unauthorized access, implementing access controls to limit who can view or modify the data, and using secure backup and disaster recovery measures to ensure that the data can be recovered in case of a security breach or other disaster.

Q14 What are the steps to reset a BIOS configuration that is password-protected?

To reset a password-protected BIOS configuration, you need to follow these steps:

1. Turn off the computer and unplug it from the power source.
2. Open the computer case and locate the BIOS battery on the motherboard.
3. Remove the BIOS battery for about 5-10 minutes to drain the power from the CMOS chip, which stores the BIOS settings.
4. Replace the BIOS battery and plug the computer back into the power source.
5. Turn on the computer and enter the BIOS configuration by pressing the appropriate key (such as F2 or Del) when prompted during the boot process.
6. The BIOS configuration should now be reset to its default settings, including password protection.

Q15 What's your preferred method of giving remote employees access to the company network and are there any weaknesses associated to it?

A common method for providing remote access to a company network is through a Virtual Private Network (VPN). VPNs allow employees to securely access the company's network from outside locations by encrypting traffic between the remote device and the company's network. However, weaknesses associated with VPNs include potential vulnerabilities in the VPN software, weak passwords, and the possibility of users losing their remote devices which could result in unauthorized access to the company's network. It is important to implement strong security measures and regularly update and maintain VPN software to mitigate these risks.

VII

SECURITY ARCHITECT

A security architect is responsible for designing and implementing an organization's security infrastructure. They work closely with other IT professionals to ensure that the company's systems and data are protected from external and internal threats. This involves identifying potential vulnerabilities in the organization's IT infrastructure, implementing appropriate security controls, and developing disaster recovery and business continuity plans. A security architect must also keep up-to-date with the latest security trends and technologies, as well as regulatory compliance requirements. They must have strong technical skills, knowledge of security frameworks, and excellent communication and leadership abilities to effectively collaborate with other stakeholders and drive security initiatives.

Chapter 7

"No technology that's connected to the Internet is unhackable."
—Abhijit Naskar

Q1 Can you provide an explanation of data leakage, and offer examples of some of the underlying causes?

Data leakage refers to the unauthorized transfer or exposure of sensitive or confidential information from a system or organization to an external entity. It can occur through deliberate actions, such as insider theft or hacking, or accidental actions, such as sending an email to the wrong recipient or leaving a document on an unsecured device. Some common root causes of data leakage include weak access controls, inadequate security policies, and human error.

Q2 Can you suggest some efficient methods to prevent data leakage?

There are several effective ways to control data leakage, including:

1. **Access controls:** Ensure that only authorized users have access to sensitive data. Use tools such as firewalls, intrusion prevention systems, and VPNs to restrict unauthorized access.
2. **Data encryption:** Encrypt sensitive data at rest and in transit. This can include using encryption algorithms to protect data while it is being

transferred, and using tools such as full disk encryption to protect data stored on devices.

3. **Employee training:** Educate employees about the importance of data protection and how to handle sensitive information. This can include training on how to recognize and report potential data breaches, as well as regular reminders about the organization's data protection policies.

4. **Data classification:** Classify data based on its sensitivity and restrict access to it accordingly. This can include implementing role-based access controls to ensure that only authorized individuals can access sensitive data.

5. **Data loss prevention (DLP) tools:** Deploy DLP tools that can monitor and prevent unauthorized data transfers. These tools can alert security teams when sensitive data is being accessed or transferred and can prevent unauthorized transfers from occurring.

6. **Network monitoring:** Monitor network traffic to detect suspicious activity and prevent data exfiltration. Use tools such as intrusion detection systems and security information and event management (SIEM) platforms to detect and respond to potential threats.

Q3 Can you explain the 80/20 rule in networking?

The 80/20 rule, also known as the Pareto Principle, is a concept in networking that suggests that 80% of the effects are caused by 20% of the causes. This rule applies to various aspects of networking, including traffic, performance, and security.

For example, in terms of traffic, 80% of the data that traverses a network typically comes from 20% of the users or applications. Similarly, in terms of performance, 80% of network performance problems can be traced back to 20% of the network devices or infrastructure.

In terms of security, the 80/20 rule suggests that 80% of security incidents are caused by 20% of the vulnerabilities or threats. Therefore, network administrators can prioritize their security efforts by focusing on the top 20% of vulnerabilities or threats that are most likely to cause security incidents.

Q4 Can you describe common vulnerabilities that web servers are susceptible to and suggest some measures to prevent web server attacks?

Web server vulnerabilities are weaknesses or flaws in web servers that can be exploited by attackers to gain unauthorized access, steal data, or disrupt the server. Some common web server vulnerabilities include SQL injection, cross-site scripting (XSS), file inclusion, buffer overflow, and command injection.

To prevent web server attacks, the following methods can be implemented:

1. Regular software updates and patching to ensure that the latest security fixes are installed.
2. Using a web application firewall (WAF) to filter out malicious traffic and attacks.
3. Implementing strong authentication mechanisms such as two-factor authentication and password policies.
4. Implementing access controls to restrict access to sensitive areas of the web server.
5. Disabling unused or unnecessary services and ports to reduce the attack surface.
6. Encrypting sensitive data in transit and at rest using SSL/TLS and other encryption protocols.
7. Regularly scanning the server for vulnerabilities and weaknesses using vulnerability scanners or penetration testing tools.
8. Implementing intrusion detection and prevention systems to detect and block suspicious activity on the web server.

Q5 Can you provide examples of the most destructive types of malware?

The most damaging types of malware include ransomware, which encrypts user data and demands payment for decryption; banking trojans, which steal financial information; and advanced persistent threats (APTs), which are sophisticated attacks designed to gain access to sensitive data over an extended period of time.

Q6 How do you typically provide remote access to the company network for employees, and what are the potential vulnerabilities or weaknesses that need to be addressed?

There are several methods to provide remote employees access to a company network, such as Virtual Private Networks (VPNs), Remote Desktop Protocols (RDP), and Cloud-based services. Each method has its strengths and weaknesses, and the choice depends on various factors such as security, performance, and cost. It is essential to implement proper security measures to avoid weaknesses such as weak passwords, unsecured networks, and unpatched vulnerabilities, which can lead to potential security breaches.

Q7 What are some network testing methods that can be used to detect security vulnerabilities?

Here are a few tests that can help identify security flaws in a network:

1. **Vulnerability scanning:** A vulnerability scan can help identify weaknesses in a network or system by searching for known vulnerabilities, misconfigurations, and outdated software.
2. **Penetration testing:** A penetration test, or pen test, is a simulated attack on a network or system to identify weaknesses that can be exploited by

attackers. This type of test can help organizations identify security flaws before they are exploited by malicious actors.

3. **Social engineering testing:** Social engineering tests are designed to identify weaknesses in an organization's human security controls. This can include testing employee awareness of phishing attacks, pretexting, or other forms of social engineering.

4. **Network traffic analysis:** Network traffic analysis can help identify suspicious network activity, including anomalous traffic patterns, unauthorized access attempts, or data exfiltration attempts.

5. **Password cracking:** Password cracking tests can be used to identify weak or easily guessable passwords, which can be a major security vulnerability.

Q8 Which types of websites and cloud services would you consider blocking?

The decision to block certain websites and cloud services depends on the organization's security policies, regulatory compliance requirements, and business needs. Typically, websites and cloud services that pose a security risk, such as those hosting malicious content or facilitating unauthorized access, should be blocked. Additionally, organizations may choose to block certain categories of websites and cloud services that are not related to work activities, such as social media, online gaming, and entertainment sites, to improve productivity and reduce the risk of security incidents.

Q9 What are some security vulnerabilities that can exist in VPNs?

While VPNs can enhance network security, they can also present security flaws. One potential flaw is the risk of a compromised VPN server, which can lead to unauthorized access to the network. Another potential flaw is a vulnerability in the VPN client software, which can be exploited by attackers to gain access to the network. Additionally, if the VPN connection is not properly configured, it may expose the network to potential threats. For example, if split-tunneling is enabled, it may allow attackers to gain access to the internet or other networks while connected to the VPN.

Q10 Explain DDoS attack?

A DDoS (Distributed Denial of Service) attack is a type of cyber attack that attempts to overwhelm a targeted website or network with a flood of traffic from multiple sources, such as botnets, compromised devices, or other systems under the control of the attacker.

The goal of a DDoS attack is to disrupt the normal functioning of the targeted system, making it unavailable to legitimate users. DDoS attacks can be difficult to defend against because the traffic appears to come from many different sources, making it challenging to block all of the malicious traffic.

Q11 Please explain the responsibilities of security operations in an organization?

The security operations team is responsible for monitoring and detecting security threats, incidents, and vulnerabilities within an enterprise's systems and networks. They work to minimize risks, respond to incidents, and maintain the security posture of the organization. Their tasks may include security monitoring, incident response, vulnerability management, threat hunting, and security awareness training.

Q12 Explain layered security architecture? Is it a good approach? Why?

Layered security architecture, also known as defense in depth, is an approach to information security that involves implementing multiple layers of security controls to protect against various types of threats. Each layer is designed to provide a different type of protection and mitigate different types of risks.

This approach is generally considered to be a good practice because it helps to reduce the risk of a single point of failure compromising the entire security posture of an organization. Even if one layer of security is breached, there are other layers in place to help prevent further damage.

However, implementing a layered security architecture can be complex and costly, and there is no one-size-fits-all approach. It requires careful planning and ongoing maintenance to ensure that all layers are working effectively together to provide the necessary protection.

Q13 Could you provide a summary of the solution you have implemented to design security measures that cover overlapping information domains?

A security solution that spans overlapping information domains typically involves implementing access controls, encryption, and network segmentation to protect sensitive data from unauthorized access. It also requires creating policies and procedures to manage the flow of data between different domains and ensuring that all systems are properly configured and maintained. This approach can be effective in reducing the risk of data breaches and improving the overall security posture, but it requires careful planning and coordination between different teams and stakeholders.

Q14 What steps do you take to incorporate the possibility of human error into a design?

To anticipate human error, I would start by conducting a thorough analysis of the design's user interface and workflow to identify potential sources of confusion or mistakes. I would then incorporate safeguards such as clear visual cues, error messages, and confirmation prompts to prevent or mitigate errors. User testing and feedback can also help refine the design to be more intuitive and user-friendly.

Q15 What steps do you take to guarantee that a design meets regulatory compliance?

To ensure that a design achieves regulatory compliance, it is necessary to research and understand the relevant regulations, standards, and guidelines, and ensure that the design adheres to them. This may involve conducting risk assessments, implementing appropriate security controls, and regularly reviewing and updating the design to ensure continued compliance. Compliance should be documented and regularly audited to ensure ongoing adherence to the relevant regulations.

Q16 Can you explain the concept of capability-based security and share any instances where you have implemented this approach in your designs?

Capability-based security is a model that provides permissions to access resources based on specific capabilities assigned to an entity, rather than relying on traditional user permissions. In this model, each capability has specific privileges and access to specific resources.

Capability-based security can be incorporated into software design by following specific principles such as defining clear, specific capabilities, and ensuring that access is restricted to only those capabilities that are necessary to perform a specific function. Additionally, it is important to ensure that capabilities are not transferred or copied to unauthorized entities to maintain the security of the system. Overall, incorporating capability-based security principles can help to mitigate security risks and improve the overall security of a system.

Q17 Can you give me a few examples of security architecture requirements?

Some examples of security architecture requirements include access control, data protection, threat detection and response, secure communication, disaster recovery, business continuity, compliance with regulatory standards, and user education and awareness.

Q18 Who typically owns security architecture requirements and what stakeholders contribute?

Security architecture requirements are typically owned by the organization's security team, which may include the chief information security officer (CISO), security architects, and security analysts. Other stakeholders who contribute to security architecture requirements may include system administrators, network engineers, application developers, compliance officers, and risk management teams.

The involvement of these stakeholders ensures that the security architecture requirements are aligned with the organization's business objectives, technology infrastructure, and regulatory requirements.

Q19 What are the unique security considerations that need to be addressed while implementing a SOA?

Service-Oriented Architecture (SOA) presents several security challenges, such as:

1. **Data protection:** In an SOA environment, data can be spread across multiple services, making it challenging to protect it against unauthorized access or modification.
2. **Authentication and authorization:** SOA environments require robust authentication and authorization mechanisms to ensure that only authorized users or services can access resources.
3. **Communication security:** Secure communication is vital in an SOA environment, as data is transmitted between services and across the network.
4. **Service availability:** SOA systems rely on multiple services, and the failure of one service can affect the availability of the entire system. Therefore, ensuring service availability and resilience is critical.
5. **Regulatory compliance:** SOA systems may have to comply with various

regulations, such as HIPAA, PCI-DSS, or GDPR, depending on the nature of the services provided and the data handled. Ensuring compliance with these regulations can be a significant challenge.

The ownership of security architecture requirements can vary depending on the organization and the project. Typically, security architects and enterprise architects lead the effort to define security architecture requirements. Stakeholders who contribute to this effort include business owners, IT leaders, security personnel, compliance experts, and application owners.

Q20 Could you elaborate on the security risks that are associated with unified communications?

Unified Communications (UC) presents several security challenges that must be addressed to ensure the confidentiality, integrity, and availability of communications. Some of the common security challenges include:

1. **Interoperability:** UC systems often integrate multiple technologies, platforms, and protocols, creating potential vulnerabilities in the communication paths.
2. **Encryption:** UC requires secure encryption of voice, video, and data communication channels to prevent unauthorized access and eavesdropping.
3. **Identity and Access Management:** As UC systems integrate multiple technologies, it is crucial to have a strong identity and access management controls to ensure authorized users access the system and its resources.
4. **Network Security:** UC systems typically rely on network infrastructure for their communication channels, making them susceptible to network-based attacks such as DDoS, Man-in-the-middle, and eavesdropping.
5. **Data privacy:** UC systems generate and store large amounts of data, including sensitive information such as customer and employee data. The security architecture must include data protection measures such as data encryption, data loss prevention, and data backup to ensure data privacy and security.

Addressing these challenges requires a comprehensive security architecture, which must be designed, implemented, and maintained by a team of security experts and stakeholders from various departments within an organization.

Q21 Do you take a different approach to the security architecture for a COTS vs a custom solution?

Yes, the approach to the security architecture for a COTS (Commercial Off-The-Shelf) solution is different from a custom solution. With a COTS solution, the security architecture is already established by the vendor, and the focus is on verifying that it meets the organization's security requirements. The organization should perform a thorough security assessment to ensure the COTS solution doesn't have any security vulnerabilities and to identify any additional security requirements that the vendor's security architecture may not cover.

On the other hand, with a custom solution, the organization has control over the security architecture from the beginning. The organization can define its security requirements and develop a security architecture that meets those requirements. The organization should also perform a security assessment to ensure that the custom solution does not have any security vulnerabilities and to identify any additional security requirements that were not previously identified.

Q22 Have you encountered any challenges while designing a security architecture that includes SaaS components?

Security challenges that may arise when incorporating SaaS components into a security solution:

One challenge with using SaaS components is that the security of the solution is partially reliant on the security of the SaaS provider's infrastructure and processes. Therefore, it is essential to assess the security capabilities of the SaaS provider before incorporating their services into a security solution. Additionally, data privacy and compliance requirements must be carefully considered when using SaaS components, as data may be transmitted and stored outside of the organization's direct control.

Another challenge may be integrating SaaS components into existing security architectures and processes. This may require changes to existing security policies, procedures, and technologies, and may involve additional configuration, monitoring, and management.

Overall, it is important to thoroughly assess the security capabilities and potential risks associated with using SaaS components and to carefully integrate them into the overall security architecture.

Q23 Describe a project where stakeholders accepted identified security risks that concerned you. How did you manage the situation?

If stakeholders choose to accept identified security risks that worry the security professional, it is important to document the risks, communicate them clearly to the stakeholders, and have them acknowledge and accept the risks in writing. It's also important to have a plan in place for monitoring the risks and addressing them if they become actual security incidents. Ultimately, the security professional's role is to advise and inform, but the decision to accept or mitigate risks lies with the stakeholders.

VIII

RISK MANAGEMENT

Risk management is the process of identifying, assessing, and prioritizing risks, followed by the coordinated and economical application of resources to minimize, monitor, and control the probability or impact of adverse events. In the context of cybersecurity, risk management is crucial for identifying and mitigating potential threats to an organization's information assets, systems, and operations. The process involves identifying and assessing the likelihood and potential impact of various threats, vulnerabilities, and risks, followed by implementing appropriate controls and countermeasures to reduce or mitigate those risks to an acceptable level. Risk management is an ongoing process, requiring constant monitoring, evaluation, and adaptation to changing security threats and business needs.

Chapter 8

Q1 Could you provide an example of a metric used to measure information security risk, and explain how risk is typically assessed?

Risk can be measured by combining the likelihood of an event with its potential impact or consequences. One example of a specific metric that measures information security risk is the annualized loss expectancy (ALE), which calculates the expected monetary loss over a one-year period due to a specific threat. ALE takes into account the probability of the threat occurring, the vulnerability to the threat, and the potential impact or cost if the threat is realized.

Q2 What is the main factor causing most companies to delay fixing their vulnerabilities?

There is no single primary reason why most companies haven't fixed their vulnerabilities, as there are many factors that can contribute to this issue. Some common reasons include a lack of resources or budget to address vulnerabilities, lack of awareness or understanding of the risks, competing priorities, and organizational silos or communication barriers.

Additionally, some companies may not prioritize security as highly as other business objectives or may view security as a compliance checkbox rather than a critical business function.

Q3 What is the objective of implementing information security in an organization?

The primary goal of information security within an organization is to protect the confidentiality, integrity, and availability of information assets. This means ensuring that sensitive and confidential information is kept safe from unauthorized access, modification, or destruction. Information security also aims to maintain the reliability and availability of IT systems and services to ensure business continuity and prevent disruption or downtime.

Additionally, information security helps to ensure compliance with legal and regulatory requirements, such as data privacy laws and industry standards. Ultimately, the goal of information security is to enable the organization to conduct its business operations securely and effectively.

Q4 Differentiate between a threat, vulnerability, and a risk?

A threat is a potential danger that can exploit a vulnerability, causing harm to an asset. A vulnerability is a weakness or flaw in a system or process that can be exploited by a threat. A risk is a likelihood that a threat will exploit a vulnerability, leading to a loss or damage to an asset, and the impact of that loss or damage.

In summary, a threat is a potential danger, a vulnerability is a weakness or flaw, and a risk is the likelihood and impact of harm resulting from a threat exploiting a vulnerability.

Q5 As a corporate information security professional, which aspect should you focus on more: threats or vulnerabilities?

As a corporate information security professional, it is important to focus on both threats and vulnerabilities. Threats are potential events that could cause harm or damage to an organization's assets, while vulnerabilities are weaknesses that can be exploited by those threats. Focusing solely on vulnerabilities could lead to a false sense of security, as the organization may not be aware of the potential threats that exist. Similarly, focusing solely on threats could lead to a reactive approach, rather than a proactive approach that addresses vulnerabilities before they are exploited.

Therefore, it is important to have a balanced approach that addresses both threats and vulnerabilities to effectively manage information security risk.

Q6 What are the main weaknesses in HTTP's design and what steps can be taken to enhance it?

HTTP, or Hypertext Transfer Protocol, is the protocol used to transfer data over the web. While it has been widely adopted and is the backbone of the internet, it has several design flaws that can lead to security vulnerabilities. Some of the primary design flaws in HTTP include:

1. **Lack of encryption:** HTTP is not encrypted by default, which means that sensitive information transmitted over the network, such as passwords and credit card numbers, can be intercepted by attackers.
2. **Lack of authentication:** HTTP does not provide a mechanism for client authentication, which means that anyone can connect to a web server and access its resources.
3. **Lack of message integrity:** HTTP does not provide a mechanism to ensure that the message sent by the client is the same as the one received by the server.

To improve the security of HTTP, several improvements have been made, such as:

1. **Encryption:** HTTPS, or HTTP Secure, uses SSL/TLS encryption to protect sensitive data in transit.
2. **Authentication:** HTTP authentication methods have been developed to allow web servers to authenticate clients.
3. **Message integrity:** HTTP message integrity can be ensured through the use of message authentication codes (MACs) or digital signatures.

In addition to these improvements, HTTP/2 has been developed to improve performance and reduce latency, and HTTP/3 is currently in development to further improve security and performance.

Q7 Explain residual risk?

Residual risk refers to the level of risk that remains after security controls have been implemented to mitigate identified risks to an acceptable level. It represents the risk that cannot be eliminated or reduced any further by implementing security measures. Residual risk exists because security controls are not foolproof, and there is always a possibility of security incidents occurring.

Q8 Differentiate between a vulnerability and an exploit?

A vulnerability is a weakness or flaw in a system's design, implementation, or operation that could be exploited to compromise the confidentiality, integrity, or availability of the system or its data. In contrast, an exploit is a specific attack that takes advantage of a vulnerability in a system or application.

In other words, a vulnerability is a weakness that an attacker seeks to exploit, while an exploit is the actual attack code or technique used to take advantage of the vulnerability. Exploits can be used to gain unauthorized access, execute malicious code, or perform other malicious actions on a system.

Q9 Is there an acceptable level of risk?

Determining an acceptable level of risk depends on various factors, such as the industry, the organization's risk tolerance, the type of data or assets being protected, and regulatory requirements. It's essential to perform a risk assessment to identify and evaluate potential threats and vulnerabilities and determine the likelihood and impact of a security incident.

Once the risk is identified, the organization can decide on the appropriate risk mitigation measures to reduce the risk to an acceptable level. However, it's important to note that completely eliminating all risks is impossible, and there will always be some level of residual risk.

Q10 Can you give me an example of risk trade-offs (e.g. risk vs cost)?

Yes, here are a few examples of risk trade-offs:

1. Choosing not to implement a security measure due to the cost of implementation and maintenance, despite the potential risk of a security breach.
2. Deciding to use a less secure but cheaper cloud service provider instead of a more secure but more expensive one.
3. Not updating software or firmware on a device because it could cause compatibility issues with other systems, despite the potential risk of a security vulnerability.
4. Allowing employees to use personal devices for work purposes to save on costs, despite the potential risk of data breaches and security incidents.

In each of these cases, there is a trade-off between the cost of implementing a security measure or taking a more secure approach and the potential risk or impact of a security incident.

Q11 Explain incident management?

Incident management refers to the process of identifying, analyzing, and responding to security incidents, breaches, or any other disruptive events that may affect an organization's systems or data. The goal of incident management is to minimize the impact of such incidents, prevent their recurrence, and recover quickly from them.

Q12 What is business continuity management? How does it relate to security?

Business continuity management (BCM) is a management process that identifies potential risks to an organization's critical functions and takes steps to ensure that these functions can continue in the event of a disruption. It includes developing plans and procedures to restore critical business functions, communications, and infrastructure following an incident.

Security is an essential component of BCM, as incidents may result from security breaches or attacks. A comprehensive BCM program includes identifying potential security threats and implementing measures to prevent or mitigate these threats. It also involves developing incident response plans to minimize the impact of security incidents on critical business functions.

Q13 Assuming that you were hired as the head engineer or CSO at a Fortune 500 company due to the previous individual's incompetence, what would be your priorities on day one, assuming that you have no prior knowledge of the organization's environment?

If I were to start a job as a head engineer or CSO at a Fortune 500 company due to the previous guy being fired for incompetence, my priorities would be:

1. **Assess the current security posture of the company:** The first step would be to perform a thorough assessment of the current security posture of the company to identify any gaps, weaknesses, and vulnerabilities that need to be addressed.

2. **Develop a comprehensive security strategy:** Based on the assessment, I would develop a comprehensive security strategy that aligns with the company's overall business goals and objectives.

3. **Build a strong security team:** I would focus on building a strong security team with the right mix of technical and non-technical skills. This team would be responsible for implementing the security strategy and ensuring that all security controls are in place and functioning properly.

4. **Enhance security awareness and training:** To ensure that all employees are aware of the importance of security, I would implement a comprehensive security awareness and training program. This program would cover topics such as password security, phishing, social engineering, and other common attack vectors.

5. **Implement a continuous monitoring program:** To ensure that the security controls are working effectively, I would implement a continuous monitoring program. This program would include regular security assessments, penetration testing, vulnerability scanning, and other testing techniques to identify any new threats or vulnerabilities.

6. **Establish a strong incident response plan:** Finally, I would establish a strong incident response plan that outlines the steps to be taken in

the event of a security incident. This plan should include procedures for identifying, containing, and remedying security incidents, as well as a communication plan to keep all stakeholders informed.

Q14 If I'm on my laptop, here inside my company, and I have just plugged in my network cable. How many packets must leave my NIC in order to complete a traceroute to twitter.com?

The number of packets required to complete a traceroute to Twitter.com from your laptop within your company's network depends on the number of network hops between your laptop and Twitter.com's server. A typical traceroute sends three packets per hop, and the number of hops can vary depending on the specific routing path taken by the packets. However, the number of packets sent per hop can be adjusted using the "-q" option in the traceroute command.

Q15 Could you suggest any improvements to the TCP protocol if you had the opportunity to redesign it?

TCP is a reliable protocol that provides connection-oriented communication and guarantees the delivery of packets. However, it has some limitations and vulnerabilities, including:

1. **Slow start:** TCP's slow-start algorithm can be a performance bottleneck for applications that require high throughput.
2. **Congestion control:** TCP's congestion control algorithm can result in unnecessary delays and decreased throughput.
3. **Security:** TCP is vulnerable to various attacks, including SYN flooding, spoofing, and injection.

If I were to redesign TCP, I would focus on addressing these issues, improving performance, and enhancing security. For example, I would explore alternative algorithms for congestion control and slow start, and incorporate stronger security measures to prevent attacks.

Q16 If you could enhance DNS with a single feature, what would it be?

A feature that can improve DNS: DNS Security Extensions (DNSSEC). DNSSEC adds a layer of security to the Domain Name System by using digital signatures to verify the authenticity of DNS data. This helps prevent DNS spoofing attacks and other types of DNS-based attacks.

Q17 In your opinion, which protocol is expected to be the dominant choice for IoT devices in the next 10 years?

It is difficult to predict the exact protocol that will be the primary one used for the Internet of Things (IoT) in 10 years as technology and trends can change rapidly. However, some experts suggest that Internet Protocol version 6 (IPv6) could be a likely candidate due to its larger address space and ability to accommodate the vast number of devices that are expected to be part of the IoT in the future. Other emerging protocols such as Bluetooth Low Energy (BLE), ZigBee, and Thread are also expected to play a significant role in connecting IoT devices.

IX

SECURITY FRAMEWORKS, ASSURANCE, AND GOVERNANCE

Security frameworks are established sets of guidelines and best practices that help organizations create and maintain robust security programs. These frameworks provide a systematic approach to security by establishing guidelines for governance, risk management, and compliance. Assurance is the process of providing confidence that an organization's security controls are working effectively. Governance is the system of policies, processes, and procedures that govern an organization's security program. Together, these concepts form the foundation of a comprehensive security strategy for any organization.

Chapter 9

"It is not data that is being exploited, it's people that are being exploited."
—Edward Snowden

Q1 Could you define Information Security Governance?

Information Security Governance refers to the set of processes, frameworks, policies, and procedures that organizations put in place to manage, monitor, and improve their information security posture. The purpose of Information Security Governance is to ensure that an organization's information assets are protected against unauthorized access, disclosure, and destruction, while also ensuring the availability and integrity of those assets.

This includes the establishment of clear roles and responsibilities for information security, the identification of information risks and the implementation of appropriate controls to mitigate those risks, and the ongoing monitoring and measurement of the effectiveness of those controls.

Q2 Could you explain the stages of the information lifecycle and how to maintain information security at each stage?

The information lifecycle consists of the creation, storage, use, transmission, and disposal of information. To ensure information security at each phase of the lifecycle, the following measures can be taken:

1. **Creation:** The creation of information can be secured by implementing access controls and enforcing strong password policies.
2. **Storage:** Information storage can be secured by encrypting data at rest, implementing access controls, and ensuring regular backups are taken.
3. **Use:** Information use can be secured by implementing user authentication controls, logging and monitoring user activity, and enforcing security policies and procedures.
4. **Transmission:** Information transmission can be secured by implementing encryption technologies, using secure communication protocols, and ensuring that all communication channels are secure.
5. **Disposal:** Information disposal can be secured by implementing secure data destruction methods and ensuring that all devices are securely wiped before disposal.

In order to ensure information security throughout the lifecycle, it is important to have a comprehensive information security governance framework that includes policies, procedures, standards, and guidelines. This framework should be regularly reviewed and updated to ensure that it is effective in mitigating emerging risks and threats.

Q3 Can you explain the concept of security controls and identify the various types of security controls?

A security control is a safeguard or countermeasure that is implemented to mitigate or reduce the risk of security threats to an information system or organization. Security controls can be technical or non-technical in nature and are designed to protect the confidentiality, integrity, and availability of information.

There are three main types of security controls:

1. **Administrative Controls:** These are policies and procedures that are put in place to manage risk and reduce the likelihood of a security incident. Examples include security policies, risk assessments, security awareness training, and incident response planning.
2. **Technical Controls:** These are controls that are implemented through technology to protect information. Examples include firewalls, encryption, access control, intrusion detection and prevention systems, and antivirus software.
3. **Physical Controls:** These are controls that are put in place to protect the physical environment where information is stored or processed. Examples include locks, access control systems, video surveillance, and environmental controls such as fire suppression systems and temperature controls.

Effective security controls are an essential component of an organization's overall security strategy and help to ensure that information is protected from unauthorized access, disclosure, and modification.

Q4 Differentiate between information protection and information assurance?

Information protection and information assurance are two related but distinct concepts in information security.

Information protection refers to the measures taken to safeguard sensitive or confidential data from unauthorized access, use, disclosure, or destruction. It involves implementing various security controls such as access controls, encryption, backup and recovery, physical security, etc. to ensure the confidentiality, integrity, and availability of data.

On the other hand, information assurance refers to the measures taken to ensure that the information system as a whole, including its hardware, software, and people, performs its intended function in a secure and reliable manner. It involves assessing and managing risks, monitoring and detecting security incidents, implementing security policies and procedures, and ensuring compliance with regulatory requirements.

In essence, information protection is focused on protecting data, while information assurance is focused on ensuring the overall security and reliability of the information system.

Q5 What is the purpose of a security policy, and why is it necessary to have one?

Security policy is a document that outlines an organization's approach to information security. It defines the rules, procedures, and guidelines that the organization must follow to ensure the confidentiality, integrity, and availability of its information assets. The purpose of a security policy is to establish a framework for managing and protecting an organization's sensitive data and intellectual property.

Q6 Explain change management?

Change management is a process that enables organizations to plan, manage, and control changes to their IT infrastructure, systems, and applications in a structured and controlled manner.

The goal of change management is to minimize the risks associated with changes to an organization's technology assets and ensure that changes are implemented in a way that minimizes disruption to the business.

Q7 Have you used any change management software or RFC tools?

Some commonly used change management software solutions in the industry include JIRA, ServiceNow, BMC Remedy, and HP Service Manager, among others. These tools help organizations to track, manage, and implement changes effectively and efficiently while adhering to the organization's change management policies and procedures.

X

SECURITY OPERATIONS & INCIDENT RESPONSE

Security Operations and Incident Response (SOIR) is the process of identifying, monitoring, detecting, analyzing, and responding to security incidents in an organization's systems and networks. SOIR aims to prevent or mitigate the impact of a security incident and to ensure that the organization's systems and networks are secure. It involves developing and implementing policies and procedures, including incident response plans, performing regular vulnerability assessments and penetration testing, and continuously monitoring for potential security threats. Effective SOIR helps organizations minimize the impact of security incidents, improve response times, and enhance overall security posture.

Chapter 10

"Security is always excessive until it's not enough."
—Robbie Sinclair

Q1 What criteria do you use to determine when an incident is considered resolved?

An incident can be considered resolved when the root cause has been identified and addressed, and all associated systems and data have been restored to their normal state or a predetermined acceptable state.

Additionally, it's important to ensure that all affected stakeholders have been notified and appropriate measures have been taken to prevent similar incidents from occurring in the future. It is also recommended to conduct a post-incident review to identify areas of improvement and implement corrective actions.

Q2 What are the steps involved in investigating a potentially infected workstation used by an employee?

Investigating a potentially infected employee workstation can be a sensitive and complex process, so it's important to handle it with care to avoid compromising any evidence or causing undue harm to the employee or the organization. Here are some general steps that could be followed:

1. **Isolate the workstation:** The first step is to isolate the workstation from the network to prevent any further damage or infection.
2. **Gather information:** Collect as much information as possible, including the nature of the incident, how it was detected, any symptoms observed, and the identity of the user.
3. **Identify the scope:** Determine the scope of the incident, including the potential damage caused, whether any data was compromised and whether the incident is limited to a single workstation or has spread to other systems.
4. **Perform a forensic analysis:** Conduct a forensic analysis of the workstation to identify any malicious files, malware, or other evidence of the infection. This should be performed by a trained and experienced forensic analyst to ensure that any evidence is properly preserved.
5. **Identify the cause:** Determine the root cause of the incident, including how the system was compromised and whether any policy violations occurred.
6. **Remediate the infection:** Once the investigation is complete, the infected workstation should be thoroughly cleaned and restored to a known good state.
7. **Educate the employee:** Provide the affected employee with guidance on how to avoid similar incidents in the future, including how to recognize potential security threats and what steps to take if they suspect their workstation has been compromised.

It's important to note that investigating a potentially infected workstation should always be done in accordance with company policies and legal requirements. The employee should be notified of the investigation, and any evidence gathered should be handled carefully to avoid violating any privacy laws.

Q3 What are the steps to take in response to a root CA breach?

A root CA (Certificate Authority) breach can be a significant security incident, as it can compromise the integrity of the entire public key infrastructure. Responding to a root CA breach requires a systematic and coordinated approach, as follows:

1. Immediately revoke the compromised root CA certificate and any other certificates that were issued based on it.
2. Analyze the root cause of the breach and take corrective actions, such as patching vulnerabilities, upgrading security controls, and improving access controls.
3. Conduct a comprehensive assessment of the scope and impact of the breach, including the number of affected systems and users, and the potential damage to confidentiality, integrity, and availability of data.
4. Notify all affected parties, including customers, partners, and regulators, and provide them with clear and timely information about the incident and the steps taken to mitigate its effects.
5. Enhance monitoring and detection capabilities to prevent similar incidents from occurring in the future, such as implementing real-time monitoring of certificate revocation lists and audit logs.
6. Develop and implement a comprehensive incident response plan that includes procedures for responding to root CA breaches, testing and refining the plan regularly, and providing regular training and awareness to employees.
7. Engage with external experts, such as forensic investigators, legal counsel, and public relations professionals, to assist with the investigation, recovery, and communication efforts.

Overall, responding to a root CA breach requires a prompt, thorough, and coordinated effort, with a focus on minimizing the impact on users, data, and systems, and preventing similar incidents from occurring in the future.

Q4 What is the procedure for analyzing netstat logs to identify potentially suspicious activities?

To analyze netstat logs for suspicious activities, follow these steps:

1. **Collect the netstat logs:** First, ensure that the netstat logs are being collected regularly. These logs contain information about active network connections, the protocol, local and remote IP addresses, and other relevant details.

2. **Review the logs:** Review the logs for any unusual activity, such as a large number of connections to a single IP address or any connections to known malicious IP addresses. Look for any open connections that shouldn't be there, and note any unusual protocols or ports.

3. **Identify the processes:** Use the PID (Process ID) listed in the netstat logs to identify the processes that are initiating the connections. This will help you determine whether the connections are legitimate or not.

4. **Check for known malicious processes:** Use a tool like Process Explorer to identify known malicious processes that may be running on the system. This can help you determine whether the connections are part of a larger malware infection.

5. **Investigate any suspicious activity:** If you identify any suspicious activity in the netstat logs, investigate it further. Look for any associated files or registry keys, and check for any other signs of compromise on the system.

6. **Take remediation actions:** Depending on the severity of the suspicious activity, take appropriate remediation actions, such as terminating the process, isolating the system, or performing a full malware scan.

Overall, analyzing netstat logs can be a useful tool for identifying suspicious activity on a network, and can help you take proactive steps to protect your systems from potential threats.

Q5 What are the steps to take in response to a server compromise?

If you suspect that a server has been compromised, it is important to take immediate action to prevent further damage and to investigate the incident thoroughly. Here are some steps you can take:

1. **Isolate the server:** Disconnect the server from the network to prevent the attacker from communicating with it and to prevent the attacker from spreading to other systems.
2. **Assess the damage:** Determine the extent of the damage and the type of attack that occurred. Review server logs and file system metadata to identify unauthorized access, changes, or other suspicious activity.
3. **Determine the root cause:** Identify the vulnerabilities that allowed the attacker to compromise the server, and take steps to remediate them.
4. **Remove the malware:** Identify and remove any malware that is present on the server, using anti-virus or anti-malware tools.
5. **Rebuild the server:** Rebuild the server from a known good backup or from a clean installation, ensuring that all software and configurations are up-to-date and secure.
6. **Monitor the network:** Monitor the network for any suspicious activity, and be prepared to take action if you detect any signs of further compromise.
7. **Notify stakeholders:** Notify relevant stakeholders such as management, customers, or regulatory bodies, as appropriate.
8. **Conduct a post-incident review:** Conduct a post-incident review to identify any gaps in security controls, update policies and procedures, and improve incident response capabilities.

It is important to have a comprehensive incident response plan in place ahead of time, including clear procedures and roles and responsibilities for each team member, to ensure an effective and efficient response to a security incident.

Q6 What steps should be taken in response to a public leak of company chat data (e.g., Slack)?

If a company's chat data, such as Slack messages, are leaked to the public, the following steps can be taken to respond to the incident:

1. **Assess the scope and impact of the leak:** Determine the extent of the leaked data, including what type of data was compromised, how much data was leaked, and who may have been affected.
2. **Notify affected parties:** Notify any individuals or groups who may have been impacted by the leak, such as employees or customers. Provide information on what data was compromised and steps they can take to protect themselves.
3. **Conduct a thorough investigation:** Conduct a thorough investigation into how the leak occurred, what caused it, and who was responsible.
4. **Take corrective action:** Once the investigation is complete, take steps to prevent future leaks, such as implementing stronger security measures or training employees on data security best practices.
5. **Be transparent:** Be transparent with stakeholders and the public about the incident, including what steps are being taken to address it and what measures are being implemented to prevent future incidents.
6. **Monitor for further leaks:** Monitor for any further leaks or indications that the leaked data is being used maliciously.
7. **Work with legal and regulatory authorities:** Work with legal and regulatory authorities, if necessary, to comply with any data protection laws and regulations and to pursue legal action against responsible parties.

Q7 What steps would you take if you become aware of a critical zero-day vulnerability that has been publicly disclosed without any available patch?

If I came to know that a critical zero-day has been disclosed without any available patch, I would immediately assess the potential impact of the vulnerability and the systems that could be affected. This would involve determining which systems are vulnerable, identifying any potential data or systems at risk, and assessing the likelihood of an attack exploiting the vulnerability.

Next, I would prioritize the patching of the vulnerability based on the severity of the issue and the potential impact on the organization. I would also consider implementing temporary workarounds or mitigations to reduce the risk until a patch is available.

In addition, I would monitor the situation closely for any updates or developments related to the zero-day vulnerability, and collaborate with relevant stakeholders, such as vendors and security researchers, to ensure the best possible response. It is also important to communicate effectively with senior management and stakeholders to ensure they are aware of the situation and can provide support if necessary.

Q8 What steps would you take if you discovered on a random Monday morning that three of the workstations' antivirus software reported removing password stealers from the system?

If three workstations are flagged as having had password stealers cleaned by their AV, it should be treated as a potential security incident. The following steps can be taken to respond to this situation:

1. Isolate the affected workstations from the network to prevent further data exfiltration or infection.
2. Collect and preserve any available evidence, such as the AV reports, system logs, and memory images, to identify the scope and impact of the incident.
3. Notify the incident response team and other relevant stakeholders, such as IT security, legal, and management, about the incident and its potential impact.
4. Conduct a thorough investigation to determine the root cause of the incident, including whether there has been a breach of sensitive information, and identify any other systems that may have been affected.
5. Apply any available patches or mitigation strategies to prevent further exploitation of the vulnerability.
6. Deploy additional monitoring and defensive measures, such as network traffic analysis and endpoint detection and response (EDR) solutions, to detect and respond to any future incidents.
7. Communicate with affected users and stakeholders about the incident, its impact, and the steps taken to remediate it. Provide guidance on how they can protect their accounts and data, such as changing passwords and enabling two-factor authentication.

Overall, a quick and effective response is critical to limit the potential damage caused by a security incident and prevent it from spreading to other systems or networks.

Q9 What information should be included in a report following a DDoS attack?

A report after a DDoS attack should include the details of the attack, such as the duration, frequency, and intensity of the traffic. It should also include the type of traffic, the target IP addresses, and the mitigation techniques used.

Additionally, it's important to include any systems or services that were impacted by the attack, the estimated cost of damages, and any recommendations for improving future security measures. The report should be detailed and comprehensive to help prevent future attacks and ensure the organization is adequately prepared for similar incidents.

Q10 If someone is trying to break into your site after analyzing the active server logs, how would you respond to this potential security incident? And should it be considered an incident?

If someone is trying to break into your site, that is indeed an incident. The following are some steps to respond to such an incident:

1. **Identify the scope and severity of the incident:** Assess the impact of the attempted intrusion, determine the number of systems involved, and whether sensitive data has been compromised.
2. **Contain the incident:** Isolate the affected systems from the network, shut down the affected services, and prevent further attempts to break in.
3. **Investigate the incident:** Collect and analyze logs and system data, and try to identify the source and nature of the attack.
4. **Mitigate the incident:** Remove any malicious software or tools used by the attacker, update the system and software to the latest version, and implement new security controls.
5. **Communicate with stakeholders:** Notify stakeholders, such as customers and vendors, of the incident, and provide updates on the status of the investigation.
6. **Learn from the incident:** Conduct a post-mortem analysis to understand what happened, what went wrong, and how the incident could have been prevented.

It's important to note that any attempted intrusion should be taken seriously, and an incident response plan should be followed to ensure the incident is contained and the security of the system is restored.

Q11 What are the methods for detecting Privilege Escalation on systems, such as *NIX, Windows, or both?

Privilege escalation is the process of obtaining elevated privileges on a system or network. It is a critical security issue that can allow attackers to gain unauthorized access and perform malicious activities. Here are some general steps that can be taken to detect privilege escalation on systems:

1. **Monitor system logs:** Check the system logs regularly to identify any suspicious activity or events that might indicate privilege escalation. Look for events related to elevated privileges or changes in user accounts, groups, or permissions.

2. **Monitor user activity:** Keep an eye on user activity and look for any signs of unauthorized access or unusual behavior.

3. **Use security tools:** Implement security tools such as intrusion detection systems, anti-virus software, and security information and event management (SIEM) solutions to detect and prevent privilege escalation attacks.

4. **Conduct vulnerability assessments:** Regularly conduct vulnerability assessments to identify any security weaknesses that could be exploited by attackers for privilege escalation.

5. **Harden system configurations:** Implement best practices for securing systems, such as disabling unnecessary services, using strong passwords, and restricting user access.

6. **Conduct regular security audits:** Conduct regular security audits to ensure that all systems and applications are secure and up-to-date with the latest patches and security updates.

In summary, detecting privilege escalation on systems requires a combination of proactive monitoring, security tools, vulnerability assessments, system hardening, and regular security audits.

Q12 What is the significance of DNS monitoring in cybersecurity?

DNS monitoring is important because DNS is a critical component of the internet infrastructure and a common target for cyber attacks. By monitoring DNS traffic, organizations can detect and prevent malicious activity such as domain hijacking, DNS spoofing, and malware propagation. DNS monitoring can also help identify and mitigate performance and availability issues.

Q13 Explain RFC?

RFC stands for "Request for Comments." It is a type of document that is published by the Internet Engineering Task Force (IETF) to describe proposed protocols, technologies, and other standards related to the Internet.

RFCs are open to public review and comment, and they are considered a primary source of information for Internet standards and best practices. They are numbered sequentially and are often cited as authoritative references for specific technical topics.

Q14 Have you ever worked in an environment that uses virtualization technology?

Virtualized environments are increasingly common in modern computing infrastructure, providing numerous benefits such as better resource utilization, improved scalability, and reduced costs. These environments use virtualization technologies such as hypervisors or containerization to create isolated virtual instances of operating systems, applications, or even entire network architectures.

In terms of security, virtualization brings some unique challenges, such as ensuring the security of virtual machine (VM) images, protecting the hypervisor and host OS from attacks, and ensuring the isolation and integrity of VMs. Security controls such as access controls, firewalls, intrusion detection, and prevention systems, and encryption can be used to mitigate these risks.

Additionally, specific virtualization security tools and techniques, such as virtual machine introspection and memory introspection, can be used to enhance security within virtualized environments.

Q15 In the event of a failed rollout, what steps do you take?

If a rollout goes wrong, the first step is to immediately notify all stakeholders, including management and technical teams involved in the rollout. The situation should be assessed and the root cause of the problem identified.

Steps should be taken to contain the issue and, if necessary, roll back any changes that were made. A post-incident review should be conducted to identify lessons learned and identify ways to prevent similar issues from occurring in the future.

Open communication with stakeholders and a proactive approach to addressing the issue are key to successfully handling a rollout gone wrong.

Q16 What is your approach to managing major incidents that affect system operations?

Managing major incidents in a system requires a well-defined incident management process that includes the following steps:

1. **Identification:** Identify and report the incident as soon as possible.
2. **Containment:** Contain the incident to prevent further damage.
3. **Analysis:** Analyze the incident to determine the root cause and extent of the damage.

4. **Eradication:** Remove the cause of the incident and eliminate the threat.
5. **Recovery:** Restore normal service as soon as possible.
6. **Review:** Review the incident and identify ways to prevent it from happening again in the future.

Effective incident management requires a clear understanding of roles and responsibilities, communication protocols, escalation procedures, and a well-defined incident response plan. It is also important to document the incident management process to ensure that it is repeatable and scalable.

Q17 When it comes to pen testing, which is more effective: a red team or a blue team?

Both red teams and blue teams are important in penetration testing.

A red team is a group of skilled security professionals who simulate real-world attacks to test the security of an organization's systems, networks, and physical security measures. The goal of a red team is to identify vulnerabilities and weaknesses that may be exploited by real attackers.

A blue team, on the other hand, is responsible for defending against attacks and maintaining the security of the organization's systems and networks. The blue team works closely with the red team to understand the attack methods and identify areas where the organization's defenses can be strengthened.

Therefore, both red and blue teams are essential in a comprehensive pen testing program. The red team helps identify weaknesses and vulnerabilities, while the blue team works on improving and maintaining the security posture of the organization.

Q18 What is the reason for hiring an external contractor to conduct a penetration test?

There are several reasons why an organization might bring in an outside contractor to perform a penetration test:

1. **Objectivity:** An outside contractor can provide an objective assessment of an organization's security posture, free from internal biases or assumptions.
2. **Expertise:** An outside contractor brings a wealth of specialized knowledge and experience in identifying security vulnerabilities and can offer recommendations for remediation.
3. **Compliance:** Many compliance regulations require periodic penetration testing, and an outside contractor can help ensure that the testing is performed correctly and meets regulatory requirements.
4. **Cost-effectiveness:** Hiring an outside contractor can be more cost-effective than hiring and training an internal team of experts.
5. **Liability:** An outside contractor can assume some of the liability associated with performing a penetration test, which can reduce the risk to the organization.

XI

SECURITY AUDITS AND TESTING

Security audits and testing are essential components of a robust security program. Audits assess the effectiveness of security controls and identify potential vulnerabilities. Testing, such as penetration testing, simulates attacks on the system to find exploitable weaknesses. Regular audits and testing help organizations to identify and address security gaps and improve their overall security posture.

Chapter 11

"Security used to be an inconvenience sometimes, but now it's a
necessity all the time."
—Martina Navratilova

Q1 What is an IT security audit?

An IT security audit is a systematic evaluation of an organization's information systems, policies, and procedures to ensure that they meet security objectives. It is conducted to identify potential vulnerabilities, assess the effectiveness of existing controls, and recommend changes to strengthen the security posture.

The audit may cover areas such as network security, access controls, data protection, and compliance with regulations and industry standards. The audit report provides a comprehensive view of the organization's security posture and helps to identify areas for improvement.

Q2 How do you test information security?

Information security can be tested through various methods such as vulnerability scanning, penetration testing, risk assessments, and security audits to ensure that systems and data are protected from unauthorized access, use, disclosure, disruption, modification, or destruction.

Q3 Differentiate between black box and white box penetration testing?

Black box and white box penetration testing are two types of security testing. Black box testing involves testing without any prior knowledge of the system being tested, simulating an external attacker.

White box testing, on the other hand, involves testing with full knowledge of the system being tested, simulating an internal attacker. The choice of testing type depends on the specific goals and objectives of the testing.

Q4 Explain the vulnerability scan?

A vulnerability scan is an automated process of identifying security weaknesses in a system or network, often using specialized software tools that search for known vulnerabilities in the system's configuration or code.

Q5 What information is typically included in a security assessment plan (security test plan)?

A security assessment plan, also known as a security test plan, outlines the scope, objectives, and methodologies of a security assessment. It typically includes a description of the systems and assets being assessed, the types of vulnerabilities and threats that will be tested, the testing approach, and the expected outcomes.

The plan may also include timelines, resource requirements, and reporting structures. Overall, the security assessment plan provides a roadmap for conducting the assessment and ensuring that it meets the organization's security objectives.

Q6 Which systems require auditing?

All systems that contain sensitive data or support critical business processes should be audited. This includes servers, workstations, network devices, databases, and applications. It is important to prioritize the systems based on their criticality and impact on the business. Additionally, systems that are subject to regulatory compliance requirements should be audited to ensure they meet the necessary standards.

Q7 In your experience, what has been the most challenging aspect of conducting audits?

The most challenging part of auditing can be identifying and documenting all relevant systems, policies, and procedures. This can be a time-consuming and meticulous process, especially in large organizations with complex IT infrastructures.

Additionally, audits require attention to detail, analytical skills, and a thorough understanding of industry regulations and best practices. The auditor must also have excellent communication skills to effectively communicate their findings to the organization's management and make recommendations for improvement.

Finally, ensuring the independence and objectivity of the audit can also be a challenging task.

Q8 Can you describe the most challenging auditing procedure you have implemented?

One of the most challenging auditing procedures involves a comprehensive review of an organization's information security controls to ensure they comply with various regulatory requirements and industry standards. This type of audit requires a thorough understanding of various frameworks, such as NIST, ISO, and COBIT.

The audit process typically involves reviewing documentation, interviewing staff, conducting vulnerability assessments, and performing penetration testing. Auditors must also have a deep knowledge of information security technologies, such as firewalls, intrusion detection systems, and encryption.

The difficulty of this audit procedure lies in the complexity and scope of the task, which requires a significant amount of time and resources. Auditors must also navigate different departments within an organization and ensure that all stakeholders are aware of the audit process and their role in it.

Q9 In what way do you request developers to document their changes?

When asking developers to document changes, it's important to make it clear why documentation is necessary and how it benefits both the developers and the organization. Here are some tips:

1. **Start with why:** Explain the importance of documentation, including how it helps the team work more efficiently, improves communication and collaboration, and reduces errors and downtime.
2. **Be specific:** Provide clear guidelines and expectations for what should be documented, including code changes, configurations, and any other relevant information.
3. **Make it easy:** Provide tools and resources that make it easy for developers

to document changes, such as templates, checklists, and documentation systems.

4. **Encourage collaboration:** Foster a culture of collaboration, where developers are encouraged to work together and share knowledge so that everyone benefits from the documentation.

5. **Provide feedback:** Review the documentation regularly and provide feedback to the developers, so they know what they're doing well and what needs improvement.

By following these guidelines, you can help ensure that your development team is documenting changes effectively, which can lead to more efficient and reliable software development.

Q10 What method do you use to compare files that may have been altered since your last review?

To compare files that might have changed since the last time you looked at them, you can use file comparison tools. These tools allow you to compare two versions of a file and identify differences between them. Some popular file comparison tools include:

1. **WinMerge:** A free and open-source tool for Windows that allows you to compare files and folders, and merge differences.
2. **Beyond Compare:** A paid tool for Windows, macOS, and Linux that allows you to compare files, folders, and even entire drives.
3. **DiffMerge:** A free tool for Windows, macOS, and Linux that allows you to compare and merge files and folders.
4. **KDiff3:** A free and open-source tool for Windows, macOS, and Linux that allows you to compare and merge files and directories.

These tools typically highlight the differences between the two versions of the file, allowing you to quickly identify changes. Some tools also provide options for merging the changes and creating a new version of the file that incorporates all the changes.

XII

ACCESS CONTROL

Access control refers to the process of regulating who or what can access specific resources or information in a system or network. It involves identifying and authenticating users and devices, authorizing them to access specific resources or perform certain actions, and monitoring and controlling access to those resources. Effective access control is critical to maintaining the confidentiality, integrity, and availability of information and preventing unauthorized access, modification.

Chapter 12

"Access control is not just about technology, it's about policy and procedure."

— **Roberta Bragg**

Q1 Differentiate between authentication and authorization?

Authentication is the process of verifying the identity of a user, device, or system attempting to access a resource or system. It ensures that only authorized users can access the resource or system.

Authorization, on the other hand, is the process of determining whether a user, device, or system has the necessary permissions to access a specific resource or perform a specific action. It determines what actions or resources the authenticated user is allowed to access.

In short, authentication is about verifying identity, while authorization is about verifying access rights.

Q2 What are the different types of information that can be utilized for authentication purposes?

There are several types of information that can be used for authentication, including:

1. **Something you know:** Examples include a password, passphrase, or PIN.
2. **Something you have:** Examples include an ID card, smart card, or mobile device.
3. **Something you are:** This includes biometric information such as fingerprint, face, voice, or iris recognition.
4. **Somewhere you are:** This refers to location-based authentication, such as GPS coordinates or IP address.
5. **Something you do:** This includes behavioral biometrics, such as the way you type, move a mouse, or use a touchscreen.

Q3 Explain role-based access control?

Role-Based Access Control (RBAC) is a method of controlling access to computer resources based on the roles and responsibilities of individual users within an organization. In RBAC, users are assigned roles, and each role has access permissions to perform specific tasks. The permissions are based on the user's job responsibilities, which are defined by the organization. This allows for more efficient management of access control and reduces the risk of unauthorized access to critical resources.

Q4 Explain the term "least privilege"?

"Least privilege" is a security principle that refers to providing users, processes, or applications with the minimum level of access required to perform their assigned tasks. This means that users are only granted access to the resources and data that are necessary to perform their job functions and nothing more.

By limiting access in this way, the risk of accidental or intentional data breaches is reduced. Additionally, if an account is compromised, the damage that can be done is limited to only the resources to which the account has access.

Q5 What is two-factor authentication? Does it require special hardware?

Two-factor authentication (2FA) is a security process that requires users to provide two forms of identification in order to access a system or application. Typically, this involves a combination of something the user knows (such as a password) and something the user has (such as a mobile phone or security token).

2FA does not necessarily require special hardware, as it can also be implemented using software-based authentication methods, such as one-time passwords (OTPs) generated through a mobile app or text message. However, some 2FA solutions do require the use of dedicated hardware tokens or smart cards.

Q6 Why are open standards important to security solutions?

Open standards are important to security solutions because they allow for interoperability and collaboration among different vendors and technologies. This ensures that security products and solutions can work together seamlessly, increasing their effectiveness and reducing the risk of vulnerabilities caused by incompatible systems.

Q7 How can conflicting requirements from different stakeholders be balanced?

Balancing demands from different stakeholders who have conflicting requirements can be challenging, but it is a critical skill in information security. One way to approach this is by understanding the priorities and concerns of each stakeholder and finding a solution that meets the needs of everyone as much as possible. It may also be helpful to establish clear communication channels and involve all stakeholders in the decision-making process to ensure that everyone's concerns are heard and addressed.

Additionally, risk assessments and cost-benefit analyses can help inform decisions and prioritize actions based on potential impact and feasibility. Ultimately, it is important to remain flexible and willing to adapt as new information or priorities arise.

XIII

CRYPTOGRAPHY

Chapter 13

"The only truly secure system is one that is powered off, cast in a block of concrete and sealed in a lead-lined room with armed guards."

— Gene Spafford

Q1 Explain secret-key cryptography?

Secret-key cryptography, also known as symmetric-key cryptography, is a cryptographic system that uses the same secret key for both encryption and decryption of the message.

Q2 Explain public-key cryptography?

Public-key cryptography, also known as asymmetric cryptography, is a cryptographic system that uses a pair of keys, a public key, and a private key, for encryption and decryption of data. The public key can be openly distributed and is used to encrypt messages, while the private key is kept secret and used for decrypting messages. It enables secure communication without the need for both parties to have the same secret key.

Q3 Explain the session key?

A session key is a symmetric encryption key that is generated and used for a single communication session between two parties. It is typically created at the start of the session, used for the duration of that session, and then discarded.

Session keys are used to encrypt and decrypt data in order to provide confidentiality and secure communication. Because they are used for only a short period of time, session keys are more secure than long-term encryption keys, which can be compromised over time. They are commonly used in secure communication protocols such as SSL/TLS and SSH.

Q4 Explain RSA?

RSA (Rivest–Shamir–Adleman) is a widely used public-key encryption algorithm that enables secure data transmission over insecure channels. RSA uses a public key for encryption and a private key for decryption. The security of the algorithm is based on the difficulty of factoring large prime numbers. RSA is used in various applications, such as secure communication, digital signatures, and secure authentication.

Q5 How fast is RSA?

The speed of RSA encryption and decryption depends on the size of the key used. With larger key sizes, RSA encryption and decryption can be computationally expensive and time-consuming. However, with smaller key sizes, it can be relatively fast.

Q6 What are the requirements or conditions necessary to break RSA?

Breaking RSA would require finding the prime factors of a very large number, which is believed to be computationally infeasible with current technology.

Q7 Is it necessary to use strong primes in RSA?

Yes, strong primes are necessary for RSA as they ensure the security and effectiveness of the algorithm. Using weak primes can make RSA vulnerable to attacks therefore, it is important to use strong primes in the generation of RSA keys to prevent potential security breaches.

Q8 What is the recommended size for RSA keys (modules)?

The size of the modulus (key) used in RSA should be chosen carefully to ensure the security of the system. Generally, the key size should be based on the required level of security, the sensitivity of the data being protected, and the expected lifetime of the system.

At a minimum, a 2048-bit key size is recommended, although 3072-bit or 4096-bit keys may be more appropriate for higher levels of security. As computing power increases over time, it may be necessary to increase key sizes to maintain the same level of security.

Q9 How large should the primes be?

The size of primes used in cryptography depends on the security level required. In general, larger primes provide higher security, and the recommended size is at least 2048 bits for RSA and 256 bits for elliptic curve cryptography.

Q10 Can you explain the practical use of RSA for authentication? Additionally, what are RSA digital signatures?

RSA can be used for authentication by employing RSA digital signatures. In this scenario, a user generates a private-public key pair, and the public key is shared with a trusted entity, like a server. When the user needs to authenticate, they create a message (e.g., a login request) and sign it using their private key. The server receives the message and the signature and verifies the signature using the user's public key. If the signature is valid, the server knows that the message was indeed sent by the user who possesses the corresponding private key.

RSA digital signatures use a mathematical function to create a message digest, which is then encrypted with the sender's private key. The receiver can then use the sender's public key to decrypt the message digest and verify that it matches the message they received. If the message digest matches, the receiver knows that the message is authentic and has not been tampered with.

Q11 What other options exist besides RSA for encryption and authentication?

There are several alternatives to RSA for public-key cryptography, including elliptic curve cryptography (ECC), Diffie-Hellman key exchange, and post-quantum cryptography (PQC) schemes like lattice-based cryptography, code-based cryptography, and hash-based cryptography.

ECC is particularly popular due to its smaller key sizes and efficient performance, making it well-suited for use in resource-constrained environments such as mobile devices and embedded systems. PQC schemes are being developed to resist attacks by quantum computers, which could potentially break RSA and other classical cryptographic systems.

Q12 Is RSA currently in use today?

Yes, RSA is currently in use today as a widely adopted and trusted public-key cryptosystem. It is used in various applications such as secure email, SSL/TLS encryption for web communication, and authentication of digital signatures.

Q13 Explain DSS and DSA?

DSS (Digital Signature Standard) and DSA (Digital Signature Algorithm) are cryptographic algorithms for creating digital signatures, which are used for authentication and verifying the integrity of digital documents. DSA is a variant of DSS and is commonly used in government and financial applications.

Q14 Differentiate between DSA and RSA?

DSA (Digital Signature Algorithm) and RSA (Rivest-Shamir-Adleman) are both used for digital signatures and authentication. The main difference is in the mathematical operations used to generate the key pairs and sign/verify messages. DSA is based on the discrete logarithm problem while RSA is based on the factorization of large primes. DSA keys tend to be smaller than RSA keys for the same level of security, but RSA is more widely used and has better support for encryption.

Q15 Is DSA secure?

DSA is considered secure when it is implemented properly with appropriate key sizes. However, like any other cryptographic algorithm, its security may be compromised in the event of mathematical breakthroughs or implementation errors. It is always recommended to use the latest and most secure algorithms and key sizes to ensure the confidentiality, integrity, and availability of sensitive data.

Q16 Explain special signature schemes?

Special signature schemes are cryptographic algorithms used for digital signatures that have specific properties and applications. Some examples of special signature schemes include:

1. **Blind signatures**
2. **Group signatures**
3. **Threshold signatures**
4. **Ring signatures**

Q17 Explain the blind signature scheme?

These are designed to allow a signer to sign a message without seeing its contents. This is useful in situations where the signer wants to maintain privacy, such as in voting systems.

Q18 Explain group signature?

These allow a group of users to collectively sign a message while keeping the identity of the individual signers anonymous. This is useful in situations where a group needs to authorize a decision, but individual members may not want to be identified.

Q19 What is blowfish?

Blowfish is a symmetric-key block cipher that was designed as a general-purpose encryption algorithm. It operates on 64-bit blocks of data and can use variable-length keys from 32 bits to 448 bits. Blowfish is widely used for the encryption of electronic data and is considered to be fast, secure, and flexible.

Q20 What is FEAL?

FEAL (Fast data Encipherment Algorithm) is a symmetric key block cipher that was designed as an alternative to DES. It operates on 64-bit blocks of plaintext and uses a 64-bit key. However, FEAL is no longer considered secure due to several weaknesses in its design, and it has been replaced by newer, more secure algorithms such as AES (Advanced Encryption Standard).

Q21 What is Skipjack?

Skipjack is a symmetric key block cipher designed by NSA. It was intended for use in various government communication systems and is classified as a Type 1 algorithm, meaning it is approved for encrypting classified information up to the Top Secret level. However, the algorithm is not widely used outside of government communications due to concerns about its security and the lack of public scrutiny it has received.

Q22 What is stream cipher?

A stream cipher is a type of encryption algorithm that processes plaintext or message bits continuously, one bit at a time, rather than in blocks like in a block cipher. Stream ciphers use a key and a pseudorandom bit stream or key stream to produce ciphertext. They are often used in applications where the amount of plaintext or data is unknown or transmitted continuously. However, stream ciphers can be less secure than block ciphers because they are vulnerable to certain types of attacks such as known plaintext attacks.

Q23 What is the advantage of public-key cryptography over secret-key cryptography?

Public-key cryptography has several advantages over secret-key cryptography:

1. **Key distribution:** In secret-key cryptography, a shared secret key needs to be distributed securely between two parties before communication can take place. This can be difficult to achieve in practice, especially over a public network. Public-key cryptography solves this problem by allowing each party to have their own public and private keys, which can be distributed freely without compromising security.

2. **Non-repudiation:** Public-key cryptography allows for non-repudiation, which means that a sender cannot deny sending a message, as their private key is used to create a digital signature that can be verified using their public key.

3. **Key exchange:** Public-key cryptography allows for secure key exchange, as each party can use the other party's public key to encrypt a shared secret key, which can then be used for further communication using a faster secret-key algorithm.

Overall, public-key cryptography offers a more flexible and secure approach to encryption than secret-key cryptography.

Q24 What is the advantage of secret-key cryptography over public-key cryptography?

The advantage of secret-key cryptography over public-key cryptography is primarily speed. Secret-key cryptography algorithms such as AES and DES are generally much faster than their public-key cryptography counterparts like RSA or DSA. Secret-key cryptography is also considered to be more secure in some situations because the keys used are typically longer than those used in public-key cryptography, and the algorithms are less complex.

Q25 Explain Message Authentication Code (MAC)?

Message Authentication Code (MAC) is a cryptographic technique used to authenticate the integrity and authenticity of a message, providing a way to detect if the message has been modified or tampered with.

Q26 What is a block cipher?

A block cipher is a cryptographic algorithm that encrypts fixed-size blocks of plaintext into ciphertext, usually with the same key. It operates on fixed-length groups of bits, called blocks, and applies a series of transformations to each block to produce an encrypted output block.

Block ciphers are commonly used to secure electronic communications, protect data at rest, and implement other cryptographic protocols. Examples of popular block ciphers include Advanced Encryption Standard (AES), Data Encryption Standard (DES), and Blowfish.

Q27 Can you provide an explanation of the various modes of operation for block ciphers in cryptography?

There are several modes of operation for block ciphers, including Electronic Codebook (ECB), Cipher Block Chaining (CBC), Cipher Feedback (CFB), Output Feedback (OFB), and Counter (CTR). Each mode offers a different way to encrypt data, with unique advantages and disadvantages. For example, CBC mode is more secure than ECB mode, while CTR mode is faster than CBC mode.

Q28 Explain the one-way hash function?

A one-way hash function is a mathematical function that takes an input (or message) of arbitrary length and produces a fixed-size output, called a hash or message digest. The key feature of a one-way hash function is that it is computationally infeasible to generate the input message from its hash value, making it suitable for digital signature schemes, password storage, and message authentication codes. Examples of commonly used one-way hash functions include SHA-256, SHA-3, and MD5.

Q29 What is collision when we talk about hash functions?

In the context of hash functions, a collision occurs when two different input messages produce the same hash value. This can compromise the integrity and authenticity of digital signatures and message authentication codes.

Q30 What are the applications of a hash function?

Hash functions have various applications in computing, including data integrity checking, digital signature generation, and password verification. They are also used in blockchain technology to generate a unique digital fingerprint of each block in the chain.

Q31 Explain the trapdoor function?

A trapdoor function is a mathematical function that is easy to compute in one direction but difficult to compute in the reverse direction unless a special value known as the trapdoor is known. The trapdoor allows for efficient computation of the reverse direction, providing a way to create cryptographic schemes such as public key encryption and digital signatures.

Q32 In cryptography, what is the primary technique for creating a shared secret over a public channel?

The main method of building a shared secret over a public medium is through the use of public-key cryptography, specifically by using the Diffie-Hellman key exchange algorithm. This algorithm allows two parties to agree on a shared secret key without ever having to exchange the key over the public channel. The parties use each other's public keys to derive a shared secret that can be used as a symmetric encryption key for secure communication.

Q33 Differentiate between Diffie-Hellman and RSA?

Diffie-Hellman and RSA are both public-key cryptographic systems, but they serve different purposes.

Diffie-Hellman is a key exchange protocol that allows two parties to securely establish a shared secret key over an insecure public communication channel. It enables two parties to exchange a secret key without explicitly sending the key over the public channel.

RSA, on the other hand, is an encryption and digital signature algorithm that can be used for secure data transmission and authentication. It involves using a public key to encrypt data, which can only be decrypted with the corresponding private key.

In summary, Diffie-Hellman is a key exchange protocol, while RSA is an encryption and digital signature algorithm.

Q34 What type of attack can exploit a standard Diffie-Hellman key exchange?

A standard Diffie-Hellman exchange is vulnerable to a man-in-the-middle (MitM) attack. In this attack, the attacker intercepts the communication between two parties and relays messages between them, such that each party believes they are communicating directly with the other party.

Q35 Differentiate between encoding, encryption, and hashing?

Encoding, encryption, and hashing are all techniques used in information security, but they serve different purposes:

- **Encoding:** This is the process of converting data from one form to another, usually to make it more suitable for transmission or storage. Encoding does not provide any security; it's just a way to represent data.
- **Encryption:** This is the process of converting plaintext (readable data) into ciphertext (unreadable data) using an encryption algorithm and a key. Encryption provides confidentiality, as only those who have the key can decrypt the ciphertext and access the plaintext.
- **Hashing:** This is the process of generating a fixed-length, unique digital fingerprint of a message or data. Hashing is used to ensure data integrity and authenticity, as any change to the data will result in a different hash value.

In summary, encoding is a way to represent data, encryption provides confidentiality, and hashing ensures data integrity and authenticity.

Q36 Differenciate between Symmetric and Asymmetric encryption?

Symmetric encryption and asymmetric encryption are two types of encryption that use different methods of key distribution and management.

In symmetric encryption, the same secret key is used for both encryption and decryption. The sender and receiver must both have access to this key in order to communicate securely. This type of encryption is fast and efficient, but key distribution can be a challenge.

Asymmetric encryption, on the other hand, uses two keys – a public key and a private key – for encryption and decryption, respectively. The public key can be freely distributed, while the private key must be kept secret. This type of encryption is slower than symmetric encryption, but key distribution is easier, making it a common choice for secure communication over the internet.

Q37 In a scenario where data needs to be both encrypted and compressed during transmission, which operation should be performed first, and what is the reason behind it?

It is recommended to compress the data before encrypting it. This is because compressing the data before encryption can improve performance and reduce the size of the encrypted data.

If encryption was performed before compression, it would be more difficult to compress the data since the encryption process would produce random-looking data that would not be easily compressed. Additionally, compression algorithms rely on patterns and redundancies in the data to achieve compression, and encryption would obscure these patterns, making compression less effective.

Q38 What is SSL and why is it not enough when it comes to encryption?

SSL (Secure Sockets Layer) is a protocol that provides secure communication between clients and servers over the internet. It uses a combination of symmetric and asymmetric encryption to encrypt the data being transmitted. While SSL provides a good level of encryption for most purposes, it is not considered to be enough for certain types of sensitive data, such as financial transactions or medical records.

This is because SSL can be vulnerable to certain types of attacks, such as man-in-the-middle attacks, where an attacker intercepts the communication and is able to read or modify the data being transmitted.

Additionally, SSL certificates can be forged or stolen, which could compromise the security of the communication. As a result, more advanced encryption methods, such as TLS (Transport Layer Security), are now commonly used instead of SSL.

Q39 Explain salting, and its use?

Salting is a technique used in cryptography to add additional randomness to data before it is hashed, typically in password storage. A salt is a random string of characters that is appended to the plaintext password before it is hashed. The purpose of salting is to prevent attackers from using pre-computed hash tables or rainbow tables to crack passwords. By adding a unique salt to each password, even if two users have the same password, their hashed values will be different, making it more difficult for attackers to crack them.

Q40 Explain salted hashes?

Salted hashes refer to the process of adding a random data string to the input of a hash function before hashing it. The random data string is known as a salt. The purpose of using salt is to prevent attackers from easily cracking hashed passwords using pre-computed hash tables or rainbow tables. By using salt, even if two users have the same password, their hashed passwords will be different because they will have different salts.

Q41 Can you provide an explanation of the Three-way handshake and how it can be exploited to carry out a denial-of-service attack?

The three-way handshake is the method used by TCP protocol to establish a connection between two devices. It involves a series of steps where the client sends a SYN packet to the server, the server responds with a SYN-ACK packet, and the client finally sends an ACK packet to complete the connection.

To create a denial-of-service (DoS) attack using the Three-way handshake, an attacker can send a large number of SYN packets to the server without responding to the SYN-ACK packets sent by the server, thereby keeping the connection half-open. This can quickly exhaust the server's resources and prevent legitimate connections from being established, leading to a denial of service. This type of attack is known as a SYN flood attack.

Q42 What's more secure, SSL or HTTPS?

SSL and HTTPS are not directly comparable, as they serve different purposes.

SSL (Secure Sockets Layer) is a security protocol used to establish a secure and encrypted connection between two endpoints, typically a client and a server.

HTTPS (Hypertext Transfer Protocol Secure) is a combination of HTTP and SSL/TLS, which encrypts data sent over HTTP using SSL/TLS protocols.

In other words, HTTPS uses SSL/TLS to encrypt HTTP traffic. So, HTTPS is more secure than HTTP because it encrypts data in transit, while SSL is just a protocol for establishing a secure connection.

Q43 Describe rainbow tables?

Rainbow tables are precomputed tables of hashes that are used to crack passwords. They are created by hashing a large number of possible passwords and storing the resulting hashes in a table. When a password hash needs to be cracked, the table is searched for a match, allowing the password to be recovered in a shorter amount of time than if the password had been brute-forced. Rainbow tables are a form of time-memory trade-off attack and are effective against hashed passwords that use weak encryption algorithms and no salting.

Q44 Differentiate between symmetric-key cryptography and public-key cryptography?

Symmetric-key cryptography is a type of encryption in which the same key is used for both encryption and decryption. It is fast and efficient but requires the key to be securely shared between the sender and receiver. Public-key cryptography uses two different keys, one for encryption and one for decryption, providing a more secure way to transmit information without needing to share the key.

Also by Shubham Mishra

Web Penetration Testing: Hack Your Way

Nothing is more important than preserving security on websites. Internet security is a constantly evolving arena, forced to improve on a daily basis as malicious attempts become more sophisticated. The sad fact is many websites lack the necessary security to protect users or owners. This should not be the case. Web Penetration Testing is a beginner's guide focusing on WordPress penetration testing. Considering how popular WordPress has become it is an attractive target for hackers. Web Penetration Testing delivers important tools every website operator needs. Filled with useful information from newbie-pleasant interface to open-source tools, this book provides the first step to ensuring your site is secure from hackers. WordPress remains one of the most popular CRM sites, making it a constant target. Can you afford to be hacked? Web Penetration Testing delivers a robust and achievable system designed to help you stop, fix, and identify hacking attempts before they steal priceless information. The internet age is the greatest advancement the world has seen to date and your security on it vital.